THIS BOOK BELONGS TO

_____

START DATE

_____

SHE READS TRUTH

EXECUTIVE

FOUNDER/CHIEF EXECUTIVE OFFICER
Raechel Myers

CO-FOUNDER/CHIEF CONTENT OFFICER
Amanda Bible Williams

CHIEF OPERATING OFFICER/
CREATIVE DIRECTOR
Ryan Myers

EXECUTIVE ASSISTANT
Mandy Raff

EDITORIAL

CONTENT DIRECTOR
John Greco, MDiv

MANAGING EDITOR
Jessica Lamb

KIDS READ TRUTH EDITOR
Melanie Rainer, MATS

CONTENT EDITORS
Matt Erickson, MATS
Kara Gause

EDITORIAL ASSISTANT
Ellen Taylor

MARKETING

MARKETING MANAGER
Kayla Stinson

COMMUNITY SUPPORT SPECIALIST
Margot Williams

MARKETING DESIGNER
Alexia Voltzow

CREATIVE

ART DIRECTOR
Amanda Barnhart

DESIGNERS
Kelsea Allen
Emily Knapp
Brandon Triola

SHIPPING & LOGISTICS

LOGISTICS MANAGER
Lauren Gloyne

SHIPPING MANAGER
Sydney Bess

FULFILLMENT COORDINATOR
Katy McKnight

FULFILLMENT SPECIALIST
Julia Rogers

SUBSCRIPTION INQUIRIES
orders@shereadstruth.com

CONTRIBUTORS

PHOTOGRAPHERS
Cedrick Jones (106)
Kylie Scruggs (81)
Cymone Wilder (Cover, 14, 40, 41,
72, 96, 109)

MODELS
Brenda Bible
Meki Clark
Nina Coyle
Sydney Harris
Hollie Keith
Andrea Miller
Natily Myers
Gabriella Paiva
Caroline Thompson
Kathleen Quiroa
Kaitlin Wernet
Cymone Wilder

@SHEREADSTRUTH
SHEREADSTRUTH.COM

SHE READS TRUTH™

© 2018 by She Reads Truth, LLC

All rights reserved.

All photography used by permission.

ISBN 978-1-949526-07-3

All Scripture is taken from the Christian Standard Bible®. Copyright © 2017 by Holman Bible Publishers. Used by permission. Christian Standard Bible® and CSB® are federally registered trademarks of Holman Bible Publishers.

Research support provided by Logos Bible Software™. Learn more at logos.com.

This book was printed offset in Nashville, Tennessee, on 70# Lynx Opaque. Cover is 100# Cougar Opaque with a soft touch lamination.

LUKE: THE GOOD NEWS

"Whether we're reading it for the first time or the fiftieth, it is always fresh, always new."

Amanda

Amanda Bible Williams
CO-FOUNDER & CHIEF
CONTENT OFFICER

The good news.

Simple though it is, you'd be surprised how long it took our team to land on that subtitle for this Luke reading plan. We circled it for weeks, tossing out idea after idea, but nothing felt quite right. We wanted a phrase that resonated but wasn't clever, one that was clear but not limiting. Most of all, we wanted it to adequately reflect the message of Jesus Christ—a message so pervasive it reframes everything else.

Midway through the process, our new content director, John Greco, joined the team. He and his wife, Laurin, had welcomed their third son into the world only a few weeks prior. The bouncing baby boy's name? Luke. The timing was not lost on any of us.

In his opening letter for He Reads Truth's Luke legacy book, John says this: "In the Bible, Luke carefully researched the life of Jesus and was so convinced of the truth of the gospel that he just had to share the good news with the world. Our prayer for our son Luke is that he, too, would so fall in love with Jesus that it spills over onto everything he touches."

This is what the gospel of Jesus does. It transforms hearts and lives. It welcomes the least and restores the broken. It replaces despair with hope. Is there any better news than this?

John's letter continues: "During my first week on the job, I read the familiar chapters of Luke's Gospel once again...I encountered the Father who loved us enough to give us His Son; the Son who endured whips and nails, scorn and shame, to save us; and the Spirit who is always at work and is promised to every believer."

The Father who loves us. The Son who died in our place. The Spirit who lives within us. This is the story Luke's Gospel tells. Whether we're reading it for the first time or the fiftieth, it is always fresh, always new. And it is always, always good.

Scattered throughout your *Luke: The Good News* book, you'll find study tools and other features to help you as you read. My favorite is the presentation of five key themes in Luke, with a fold-out key you can customize and keep open as you read. At the end of your study, you'll have the opportunity to go back through your notes and reflect on what God has taught you about the Holy Spirit, prayer, faith, joy, and God's kingdom.

May God meet you in these pages as you read the good news of God's love for you.

"Never[t]
when th[e]
of Man
will he fi[nd]
[f]aith on

We used
masking tape
as a nod to
the way Luke
pieced together
eyewitness
accounts.

The Baskerville
typeface is
reminiscent of
old newspaper
headlines and
long-form stories.

Baskervi[lle]
Abcdefghijk[l]
1234567890[1]

PANTONE
PANTONE

Foliage throughout
the book reminds us
that Jesus walked
the earth in real
space and time.

We photographed
a diverse group of
Shes to represent
the diverse range of
people Jesus came
to serve.

DESIGN ON PURPOSE

She Reads Truth is a community of women dedicated to reading the Word of God every day.

The Bible is living and active, breathed out by God, and we confidently hold it higher than anything we can do or say. This book focuses primarily on Scripture, with bonus resources to facilitate deeper engagement with God's Word.

SCRIPTURE READING

This study book presents the book of Luke in daily readings, with supplemental passages for additional context.

JOURNALING SPACE

Each weekday features space for personal reflection and prayer.

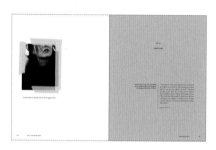

GRACE DAY

Use Saturdays to pray, rest, and reflect on what you've read.

WEEKLY TRUTH

Sundays are set aside for weekly Scripture memorization.

Find the corresponding memory cards in the back of this book.

EXTRAS

This book features additional tools to help you gain a deeper understanding of the text.

Luke — 5 Weeks

PLAN OVERVIEW ^

"For the Son of Man has come to seek and to save the lost." This is the message of the Gospel of Luke, a detailed account of the life and ministry of Jesus, from His birth in Bethlehem to His ascension into heaven. As we read through this five-week plan, pay close attention to Jesus seeking out the marginalized and engaging the religious leaders of the day. Watch Him minister in the power of the Holy Spirit, praying at key points in the narrative. Listen as He teaches

For added community and conversation, join us in the **Luke** reading plan on the She Reads Truth app or at SheReadsTruth.com.

Themes in Luke PAGE 18
FOLD-OUT

Prophecies of Jesus's Birth PAGE 26

Why Are There Four Gospels? PAGE 93

Jesus's Post-Resurrection Appearances PAGE 160

Themes in Luke: Reflection PAGE 166

Jesus and the Marginalized

PAGE 60

Jesus often ministered to people considered outsiders, or even outcasts, by society.

Parables Unique to Luke

PAGE 118

Learn about the parables only found in the Gospel of Luke.

Daily Reading

WEEK ONE

DAY 1	The Coming Savior	20
DAY 2	The Birth of Jesus	28
DAY 3	The Messiah's Herald	33
DAY 4	Jesus's Early Ministry	36
DAY 5	The First Disciples	42
DAY 6	Grace Day	47
DAY 7	Weekly Truth	48

WEEK 2

DAY 8	Lord of the Sabbath	50
DAY 9	Much Forgiveness, Much Love	54
DAY 10	Parables and Miracles	64
DAY 11	Take Up Your Cross	69
DAY 12	In His Name	74
DAY 13	Grace Day	79
DAY 14	Weekly Truth	80

CONTINUED

TABLE OF CONTENTS

WEEK 3

DAY 15	The Son Reveals the Father	82
DAY 16	True Blessedness	86
DAY 17	Acknowledging Christ	90
DAY 18	The Narrow Way	98
DAY 19	Teachings on Humility	103
DAY 20	Grace Day	107
DAY 21	Weekly Truth	108

WEEK 4

DAY 22	Lost and Found	111
DAY 23	Kingdom Values	114
DAY 24	Faith and Duty	120
DAY 25	Entering the Kingdom	125
DAY 26	The Triumphal Entry	128
DAY 27	Grace Day	133
DAY 28	Weekly Truth	134

WEEK 5

DAY 29	The Authority of Jesus Challenged	137
DAY 30	The Coming of the Son of Man	142
DAY 31	The Plot to Kill Jesus	146
DAY 32	The Death of Jesus	152
DAY 33	The Reality of the Risen Jesus	156
DAY 34	Grace Day	163
DAY 35	Weekly Truth	164

The gospel is neither a discussion nor a debate.
It is an announcement.

DR. PAUL S. REES

ON THE TIMELINE

The third Gospel is commonly believed to have been written by the same author, and around the same time, as the book of Acts. Considerable evidence points to Luke as the writer of both books, including Acts 1:1–3, which identifies Acts as a sequel to Luke. The events at the end of Acts occurred around AD 62–63, indicating that both Luke and Acts were most likely written in the early to mid 60s. The events of the Gospel of Luke occur around the life of Christ, from about 5 BC to AD 33.

A LITTLE BACKGROUND

Like Acts, Luke's Gospel is addressed to "most honorable Theophilus" (Lk 1:3), about whom nothing else is known. The Greek name Theophilus means "lover of God" and implies he was a Gentile, probably Greek. He seems to have been a relatively new believer, recently instructed about Jesus and the Christian faith. Luke's profession as a medical doctor gives his Gospel a unique focus on Jesus's humanity and the role of Christ as the Suffering Servant (Is 53).

MESSAGE & PURPOSE

The Gospel of Luke is a carefully researched (Lk 1:3) and selective presentation of the person and life of Jesus Christ. The book is designed to strengthen the faith of believers (Lk 1:3–4) and challenge the misconceptions of unbelievers, especially those from a Greek background. Luke's Gospel is a well-balanced portrait of Jesus, skillfully emphasizing His divinity and perfect humanity.

GIVE THANKS FOR THE GOSPEL OF LUKE

Some thirty-five percent of the material in the Gospel of Luke is unique, so there is a great deal we would not know if this book had not been included in the Bible. These distinct passages include the births of John the Baptist and Jesus (Lk 2–3), the retellings of Jesus's childhood and pre-ministry adult life (Lk 2:40–52), a genealogy that emphasizes different aspects of Jesus's ancestry than the genealogy in Matthew (Lk 1:1–17), additional information about Jesus's journey to Jerusalem (Lk 9:51–19:44), and a different take on the destruction of the temple (Lk 21:5–38). Also specific to Luke are the account of the Emmaus Road and the only description in the Gospels of Jesus's ascension into heaven (Lk 24:13–53).

KEY VERSE: LUKE 19:10

"For the Son of Man has come to seek and to save the lost."

KEEP YOUR KEY OPEN AS YOU
READ FOR EASY REFERENCE!

The Holy Spirit, prayer, faith, joy, and the kingdom of God are all key themes in the Gospel of Luke. To help you identify these themes as you read, we've included this quick-reference guide with space for you to create your own key for marking each theme in the text.

At the end of this study, use the space provided on page 166 to revisit your notes and reflect on these themes from Luke's Gospel.

STUDY KEY

Create your own key below. For example, you might choose to highlight each theme in a specific color or place a unique symbol in the margin.

THE PRESENCE OF THE **HOLY SPIRIT**

PRAYER AND TEACHING ON PRAYER

THE IMPORTANCE OF **FAITH**

JOY IN GOD'S SALVATION

THE **KINGDOM** OF GOD

Themes
in Luke

1 The presence of the Holy Spirit

2 Prayer and teaching on prayer

3 The importance of faith

4 Joy in God's salvation

5 The kingdom of God

The Coming Savior

THE DEDICATION TO THEOPHILUS

¹ Many have undertaken to compile a narrative about the events that have been fulfilled among us, ² just as the original eyewitnesses and servants of the word handed them down to us. ³ It also seemed good to me, since I have carefully investigated everything from the very first, to write to you in an orderly sequence, most honorable Theophilus, ⁴ so that you may know the certainty of the things about which you have been instructed.

GABRIEL PREDICTS JOHN'S BIRTH

⁵ In the days of King Herod of Judea, there was a priest of Abijah's division named Zechariah. His wife was from the daughters of Aaron, and her name was Elizabeth. ⁶ Both were righteous in God's sight, living without blame according to all the commands and requirements of the Lord. ⁷ But they had no children because Elizabeth could not conceive, and both of them were well along in years.

⁸ When his division was on duty and he was serving as priest before God, ⁹ it happened that he was chosen by lot, according to the custom of the priesthood, to enter the sanctuary of the Lord and burn incense. ¹⁰ At the hour of incense the whole assembly of the people was praying outside. ¹¹ An angel of the Lord appeared to him, standing to the right of the altar of incense. ¹² When Zechariah saw him, he was terrified and overcome with fear. ¹³ But the angel said to him: "Do not be afraid, Zechariah, because your prayer has been heard. Your wife Elizabeth will bear you a son, and you will name him John. ¹⁴ There will be joy and delight for you, and many will rejoice at his birth. ¹⁵ For he will be great in the sight of the Lord and will never drink wine or beer. He will be filled with the Holy Spirit while still in his mother's womb. ¹⁶ He will turn many of the children of Israel to the Lord their God. ¹⁷ And he will go before him in the spirit and power of Elijah, to turn the hearts of fathers to their children, and the disobedient to the understanding of the righteous, to make ready for the Lord a prepared people."

¹⁸ "How can I know this?" Zechariah asked the angel. "For I am an old man, and my wife is well along in years."

¹⁹ The angel answered him, "I am Gabriel, who stands in the presence of God, and I was sent to speak to you and tell you this good news. ²⁰ Now listen. You will become silent and unable to speak until the day these things take place, because you did not believe my words, which will be fulfilled in their proper time."

²¹ Meanwhile, the people were waiting for Zechariah, amazed that he stayed so long in the sanctuary. ²² When he did come out, he could not speak to them. Then they realized that he had seen a vision in the sanctuary. He was making signs to them and remained speechless. ²³ When the days of his ministry were completed, he went back home.

²⁴ After these days his wife Elizabeth conceived and kept herself in seclusion for five months. She said, ²⁵ "The Lord has done this for me. He has looked with favor in these days to take away my disgrace among the people."

GABRIEL PREDICTS JESUS'S BIRTH

²⁶ In the sixth month, the angel Gabriel was sent by God to a town in Galilee called Nazareth, ²⁷ to a virgin engaged to a man named Joseph, of the house of David. The virgin's name was Mary. ²⁸ And the angel came to her and said, "Greetings, favored woman! The Lord is with you." ²⁹ But she was deeply troubled by this statement, wondering what kind of greeting this could be. ³⁰ Then the angel told her: "Do not be afraid, Mary, for you have found favor with God. ³¹ Now listen: You will conceive and give birth to a son, and you will name him Jesus. ³² He will be great and will be called the Son of the Most High, and the Lord God will give him the throne of his father David. ³³ He will reign over the house of Jacob forever, and his kingdom will have no end."

³⁴ Mary asked the angel, "How can this be, since I have not had sexual relations with a man?"

³⁵ The angel replied to her: "The Holy Spirit will come upon you, and the power of the Most High will overshadow you. Therefore, the holy one to be born will be called the Son

of God. ³⁶ "And consider your relative Elizabeth—even she has conceived a son in her old age, and this is the sixth month for her who was called childless. ³⁷ For nothing will be impossible with God."

³⁸ "I am the Lord's servant," said Mary. "May it be done to me according to your word." Then the angel left her.

MARY'S VISIT TO ELIZABETH

³⁹ In those days Mary set out and hurried to a town in the hill country of Judah ⁴⁰ where she entered Zechariah's house and greeted Elizabeth. ⁴¹ When Elizabeth heard Mary's greeting, the baby leaped inside her, and Elizabeth was filled with the Holy Spirit. ⁴² Then she exclaimed with a loud cry: "Blessed are you among women, and your child will be blessed! ⁴³ How could this happen to me, that the mother of my Lord should come to me? ⁴⁴ For you see, when the sound of your greeting reached my ears, the baby leaped for joy inside me. ⁴⁵ Blessed is she who has believed that the Lord would fulfill what he has spoken to her!"

MARY'S PRAISE

⁴⁶ And Mary said:

My soul praises the greatness of the Lord,
⁴⁷ and my spirit rejoices in God my Savior,
⁴⁸ because he has looked with favor
on the humble condition of his servant.
Surely, from now on all generations
will call me blessed,
⁴⁹ because the Mighty One
has done great things for me,
and his name is holy.
⁵⁰ His mercy is from generation to generation
on those who fear him.
⁵¹ He has done a mighty deed with his arm;
he has scattered the proud
because of the thoughts of their hearts;
⁵² he has toppled the mighty from their thrones
and exalted the lowly.
⁵³ He has satisfied the hungry with good things
and sent the rich away empty.
⁵⁴ He has helped his servant Israel,
remembering his mercy

⁵⁵ to Abraham and his descendants forever,
just as he spoke to our ancestors.

⁵⁶ And Mary stayed with her about three months; then she returned to her home.

THE BIRTH AND NAMING OF JOHN

⁵⁷ Now the time had come for Elizabeth to give birth, and she had a son. ⁵⁸ Then her neighbors and relatives heard that the Lord had shown her his great mercy, and they rejoiced with her.

⁵⁹ When they came to circumcise the child on the eighth day, they were going to name him Zechariah, after his father. ⁶⁰ But his mother responded, "No. He will be called John."

⁶¹ Then they said to her, "None of your relatives has that name." ⁶² So they motioned to his father to find out what he wanted him to be called. ⁶³ He asked for a writing tablet and wrote: "His name is John." And they were all amazed. ⁶⁴ Immediately his mouth was opened and his tongue set free, and he began to speak, praising God. ⁶⁵ Fear came on all those who lived around them, and all these things were being talked about throughout the hill country of Judea. ⁶⁶ All who heard about him took it to heart, saying, "What then will this child become?" For, indeed, the Lord's hand was with him.

ZECHARIAH'S PROPHECY

⁶⁷ Then his father Zechariah was filled with the Holy Spirit and prophesied:

⁶⁸ Blessed is the Lord, the God of Israel,
because he has visited
and provided redemption for his people.
⁶⁹ He has raised up a horn of salvation for us
in the house of his servant David,
⁷⁰ just as he spoke by the mouth
of his holy prophets in ancient times;
⁷¹ salvation from our enemies
and from the hand of those who hate us.
⁷² He has dealt mercifully with our fathers
and remembered his holy covenant—
⁷³ the oath that he swore to our father Abraham.

He has given us the privilege,
[74] since we have been rescued
from the hand of our enemies,
to serve him without fear
[75] in holiness and righteousness
in his presence all our days.
[76] And you, child, will be called
a prophet of the Most High,
for you will go before the Lord
to prepare his ways,
[77] to give his people knowledge of salvation
through the forgiveness of their sins.
[78] Because of our God's merciful compassion,
the dawn from on high will visit us
[79] to shine on those who live in darkness
and the shadow of death,
to guide our feet into the way of peace.

[80] The child grew up and became spiritually strong, and he was in the wilderness until the day of his public appearance to Israel.

1 Samuel 2:1–10
HANNAH'S TRIUMPHANT PRAYER

[1] Hannah prayed:

My heart rejoices in the LORD;
my horn is lifted up by the LORD.
My mouth boasts over my enemies,
because I rejoice in your salvation.
[2] There is no one holy like the LORD.
There is no one besides you!
And there is no rock like our God.
[3] Do not boast so proudly,
or let arrogant words come out of your mouth,
for the LORD is a God of knowledge,
and actions are weighed by him.
[4] The bows of the warriors are broken,
but the feeble are clothed with strength.
[5] Those who are full hire themselves out for food,
but those who are starving hunger no more.
The woman who is childless gives birth to seven,
but the woman with many sons pines away.

[6] The LORD brings death and gives life;
he sends some down to Sheol, and he raises others up.
[7] The LORD brings poverty and gives wealth;
he humbles and he exalts.
[8] He raises the poor from the dust
and lifts the needy from the trash heap.
He seats them with noblemen
and gives them a throne of honor.
For the foundations of the earth are the LORD's;
he has set the world on them.
[9] He guards the steps of his faithful ones,
but the wicked perish in darkness,
for a person does not prevail by his own strength.
[10] Those who oppose the LORD will be shattered;
he will thunder in the heavens against them.
The LORD will judge the ends of the earth.
He will give power to his king;
he will lift up the horn of his anointed.

Jeremiah 23:5–6
THE RIGHTEOUS BRANCH OF DAVID

[5] "Look, the days are coming"—this is the LORD's
    declaration—
"when I will raise up a Righteous Branch for David.
He will reign wisely as king
and administer justice and righteousness in the land.

[6] In his days Judah will be saved,
and Israel will dwell securely.
This is the name he will be called:
The LORD Is Our Righteousness.

NOTES

Prophecies of Jesus's Birth

From Genesis to Malachi, the Old Testament contains many prophecies about the Messiah. Below are some of these Old Testament prophecies, along with their New Testament fulfillments and references for each.

In his days Judah will be saved, and Israel will dwell securely. This is the name he will be called: The LORD Is Our Righteousness.

JR 23:6

See, the virgin will conceive, have a son, and name him Immanuel.

IS 7:14

CALLED "LORD"

Therefore, the LORD himself will give you a sign: See, the virgin will conceive, have a son...

IS 7:14

CALLED "IMMANUEL"

LK 2:11

Today in the city of David a Savior was born for you, who is the Messiah, the Lord.

I will declare the LORD's decree. He said to me, "You are my Son; today I have become your Father."

PS 2:7

BORN OF A VIRGIN

MT 1:22–23

Now all this took place to fulfill what was spoken by the Lord through the prophet: See, the virgin... will name him Immanuel, which is translated "God is with us."

"I will put hostility between you and the woman, and between your offspring and her offspring. He will strike your head, and you will strike his heel."

THE SON OF GOD

LK 1:26–27

Old Testament Prophecy — GN 3:15

THE SON OF MAN

LK 3:22

The Savior will be...

Fulfilled in Christ — GL 4:4

When the time came to completion, God sent his Son, born of a woman, born under the law...

...and the Holy Spirit descended on him in a physical appearance like a dove. And a voice came from heaven: "You are my beloved Son; with you I am well-pleased."

In the sixth month, the angel Gabriel was sent by God to a town in Galilee called Nazareth, to a virgin engaged to a man named Joseph, of the house of David. The virgin's name was Mary.

This is what the LORD says:

A voice was
heard in Ramah,
a lament with
bitter weeping—
Rachel weeping
for her children,
refusing to be
comforted for her
children because
they are no more.

JR 31:15

"When your time
comes and you
rest with your
fathers, I will raise
up after you your
descendant, who
will come from
your body, and I
will establish his
kingdom. He is
the one who will
build a house for
my name, and
I will establish
the throne of his
kingdom forever."

Bethlehem
Ephrathah, you
are small among
the clans of
Judah; one will
come from you
to be ruler over
Israel for me. His
origin is from
antiquity, from
ancient times.

When Israel was
a child, I loved
him, and out of
Egypt I called
my son.

HS 11:1

BORN INTO SORROW

MC 5:2

2SM 7:12–13

CALLED OUT OF EGYPT

MT 2:16–17

BORN IN BETHLEHEM

MT 2:14–15

I see him, but not
now; I perceive
him, but not near.
A star will come
from Jacob, and
a scepter will
arise from Israel.

NM 24:17

ON KING DAVID'S THRONE FOREVER

MT 2:3–5

So he got up,
took the child
and his mother
during the night,
and escaped
to Egypt. He
stayed there until
Herod's death,
so that what was
spoken by the
Lord through the
prophet might be
fulfilled: Out of
Egypt I called
my Son.

Then Herod,
when he realized
that he had been
outwitted by the
wise men, flew
into a rage. He
gave orders
to massacre
all the boys in
and around
Bethlehem who
were two years
old and under,
in keeping with
the time he had
learned from the
wise men. Then
what was spoken
through Jeremiah
the prophet was
fulfilled.

"And all the
nations of the
earth will be
blessed by your
offspring because
you have obeyed
my command."

GN 22:18

THE STAR OF JACOB

LK 1:32

LK 1:33

He will be great
and will be called
the Son of the
Most High, and
the Lord God
will give him
the throne of his
father David.

When King Herod
heard this, he was
deeply disturbed,
and all Jerusalem
with him. So he
assembled all
the chief priests
and scribes of
the people and
asked them
where the Christ
would be born.
"In Bethlehem of
Judea," they told
him…

FROM THE LINE OF ABRAHAM

He will reign
over the house
of Jacob forever,
and his kingdom
will have no end.

MT 1:1–2

An account of
the genealogy of
Jesus Christ, the
Son of David, the
Son of Abraham:
Abraham
fathered Isaac…

The Birth of Jesus

Luke 2

THE BIRTH OF JESUS

[1] In those days a decree went out from Caesar Augustus that the whole empire should be registered. [2] This first registration took place while Quirinius was governing Syria. [3] So everyone went to be registered, each to his own town.

[4] Joseph also went up from the town of Nazareth in Galilee, to Judea, to the city of David, which is called Bethlehem, because he was of the house and family line of David, [5] to be registered along with Mary, who was engaged to him and was pregnant. [6] While they were there, the time came for her to give birth. [7] Then she gave birth to her firstborn son, and she wrapped him tightly in cloth and laid him in a manger, because there was no guest room available for them.

THE SHEPHERDS AND THE ANGELS

[8] In the same region, shepherds were staying out in the fields and keeping watch at night over their flock. [9] Then an angel of the Lord stood before them, and the glory of the Lord shone around them, and they were terrified. [10] But the angel said to them, "Don't be afraid, for look, I proclaim to you good news of great joy that will be for all the people: [11] Today in the city of David a Savior was born for you, who is the Messiah, the Lord. [12] This will be the sign for you: You will find a baby wrapped tightly in cloth and lying in a manger."

[13] Suddenly there was a multitude of the heavenly host with the angel, praising God and saying:

> [14] Glory to God in the highest heaven,
> and peace on earth to people he favors!

[15] When the angels had left them and returned to heaven, the shepherds said to one another, "Let's go straight to Bethlehem and see what has happened, which the Lord has made known to us."

[16] They hurried off and found both Mary and Joseph, and the baby who was lying in the manger. [17] After seeing them, they reported the message they were told about this child, [18] and all who heard it were amazed at what the shepherds said to them. [19] But Mary was treasuring up all these things in her heart and meditating on them. [20] The shepherds

returned, glorifying and praising God for all the things they had seen and heard, which were just as they had been told.

THE CIRCUMCISION AND PRESENTATION OF JESUS

[21] When the eight days were completed for his circumcision, he was named Jesus—the name given by the angel before he was conceived. [22] And when the days of their purification according to the law of Moses were finished, they brought him up to Jerusalem to present him to the Lord [23] (just as it is written in the law of the Lord, Every firstborn male will be dedicated to the Lord) [24] and to offer a sacrifice (according to what is stated in the law of the Lord, a pair of turtledoves or two young pigeons).

SIMEON'S PROPHETIC PRAISE

[25] There was a man in Jerusalem whose name was Simeon. This man was righteous and devout, looking forward to Israel's consolation, and the Holy Spirit was on him. [26] It had been revealed to him by the Holy Spirit that he would not see death before he saw the Lord's Messiah. [27] Guided by the Spirit, he entered the temple. When the parents brought in the child Jesus to perform for him what was customary under the law, [28] Simeon took him up in his arms, praised God, and said,

> [29] Now, Master,
> you can dismiss your servant in peace,
> as you promised.
> [30] For my eyes have seen your salvation.
> [31] You have prepared it
> in the presence of all peoples—
> [32] a light for revelation to the Gentiles
> and glory to your people Israel.

[33] His father and mother were amazed at what was being said about him. [34] Then Simeon blessed them and told his mother Mary: "Indeed, this child is destined to cause the fall and rise of many in Israel and to be a sign that will be opposed— [35] and a sword will pierce your own soul—that the thoughts of many hearts may be revealed."

ANNA'S TESTIMONY

[36] There was also a prophetess, Anna, a daughter of Phanuel, of the tribe of Asher. She was well along in years, having lived

with her husband seven years after her marriage, [37] and was a widow for eighty-four years. She did not leave the temple, serving God night and day with fasting and prayers. [38] At that very moment, she came up and began to thank God and to speak about him to all who were looking forward to the redemption of Jerusalem.

THE FAMILY'S RETURN TO NAZARETH

[39] When they had completed everything according to the law of the Lord, they returned to Galilee, to their own town of Nazareth. [40] The boy grew up and became strong, filled with wisdom, and God's grace was on him.

IN HIS FATHER'S HOUSE

[41] Every year his parents traveled to Jerusalem for the Passover Festival. [42] When he was twelve years old, they went up according to the custom of the festival. [43] After those days were over, as they were returning, the boy Jesus stayed behind in Jerusalem, but his parents did not know it. [44] Assuming he was in the traveling party, they went a day's journey. Then they began looking for him among their relatives and friends. [45] When they did not find him, they returned to Jerusalem to search for him. [46] After three days, they found him in the temple sitting among the teachers, listening to them and asking them questions. [47] And all those who heard him were astounded at his understanding and his answers. [48] When his parents saw him, they were astonished, and his mother said to him, "Son, why have you treated us like this? Your father and I have been anxiously searching for you."

[49] "Why were you searching for me?" he asked them. "Didn't you know that it was necessary for me to be in my Father's house?" [50] But they did not understand what he said to them.

IN FAVOR WITH GOD AND WITH PEOPLE

[51] Then he went down with them and came to Nazareth and was obedient to them. His mother kept all these things in her heart. [52] And Jesus increased in wisdom and stature, and in favor with God and with people.

Isaiah 9:2–7

[2] The people walking in darkness
have seen a great light;
a light has dawned
on those living in the land of darkness.
[3] You have enlarged the nation
and increased its joy.
The people have rejoiced before you
as they rejoice at harvest time
and as they rejoice when dividing spoils.
[4] For you have shattered their oppressive yoke
and the rod on their shoulders,
the staff of their oppressor,
just as you did on the day of Midian.
[5] For every trampling boot of battle
and the bloodied garments of war
will be burned as fuel for the fire.
[6] For a child will be born for us,
a son will be given to us,
and the government will be on his shoulders.
He will be named
Wonderful Counselor, Mighty God,
Eternal Father, Prince of Peace.
[7] The dominion will be vast,
and its prosperity will never end.
He will reign on the throne of David
and over his kingdom,
to establish and sustain it
with justice and righteousness from now on and forever.
The zeal of the LORD of Armies will accomplish this.

Galatians 4:4–5

[4] When the time came to completion, God sent his Son, born of a woman, born under the law, [5] to redeem those under the law, so that we might receive adoption as sons.

NOTES   *date*

One who
is more
powerful
than I am
is coming.

Luke 3:16

THE MESSIAH'S HERALD

Luke 3

THE MESSIAH'S HERALD

¹ In the fifteenth year of the reign of Tiberius Caesar, while Pontius Pilate was governor of Judea, Herod was tetrarch of Galilee, his brother Philip tetrarch of the region of Iturea and Trachonitis, and Lysanias tetrarch of Abilene, ² during the high priesthood of Annas and Caiaphas, God's word came to John the son of Zechariah in the wilderness. ³ He went into all the vicinity of the Jordan, proclaiming a baptism of repentance for the forgiveness of sins, ⁴ as it is written in the book of the words of the prophet Isaiah:

A voice of one crying out in the wilderness:
Prepare the way for the Lord;
make his paths straight!
⁵ Every valley will be filled,
and every mountain and hill will be made low;
the crooked will become straight,
the rough ways smooth,
⁶ and everyone will see the salvation of God.

⁷ He then said to the crowds who came out to be baptized by him, "Brood of vipers! Who warned you to flee from the coming wrath? ⁸ Therefore produce fruit consistent with repentance. And don't start saying to yourselves, 'We have Abraham as our father,' for I tell you that God is able to raise up children for Abraham from these stones. ⁹ The ax is already at the root of the trees. Therefore, every tree that doesn't produce good fruit will be cut down and thrown into the fire."

¹⁰ "What then should we do?" the crowds were asking him.

¹¹ He replied to them, "The one who has two shirts must share with someone who has none, and the one who has food must do the same."

¹² Tax collectors also came to be baptized, and they asked him, "Teacher, what should we do?"

¹³ He told them, "Don't collect any more than what you have been authorized."

¹⁴ Some soldiers also questioned him, "What should we do?"

He said to them, "Don't take money from anyone by force or false accusation, and be satisfied with your wages."

¹⁵ Now the people were waiting expectantly, and all of them were questioning in their hearts whether John might be the Messiah. ¹⁶ John answered them all, "I baptize you with water, but one who is more powerful than I am is coming.

I am not worthy to untie the strap of his sandals. He will baptize you with the Holy Spirit and fire. [17] His winnowing shovel is in his hand to clear his threshing floor and gather the wheat into his barn, but the chaff he will burn with fire that never goes out." [18] Then, along with many other exhortations, he proclaimed good news to the people. [19] But when John rebuked Herod the tetrarch because of Herodias, his brother's wife, and all the evil things he had done, [20] Herod added this to everything else—he locked up John in prison.

THE BAPTISM OF JESUS

[21] When all the people were baptized, Jesus also was baptized. As he was praying, heaven opened, [22] and the Holy Spirit descended on him in a physical appearance like a dove. And a voice came from heaven: "You are my beloved Son; with you I am well-pleased."

THE GENEALOGY OF JESUS CHRIST

[23] As he began his ministry, Jesus was about thirty years old and was thought to be the

son of Joseph, son of Heli,
[24] son of Matthat, son of Levi,
son of Melchi, son of Jannai,
son of Joseph, [25] son of Mattathias,
son of Amos, son of Nahum,
son of Esli, son of Naggai,
[26] son of Maath, son of Mattathias,
son of Semein, son of Josech,
son of Joda, [27] son of Joanan,
son of Rhesa, son of Zerubbabel,
son of Shealtiel, son of Neri,
[28] son of Melchi, son of Addi,
son of Cosam, son of Elmadam,
son of Er, [29] son of Joshua,
son of Eliezer, son of Jorim,
son of Matthat, son of Levi,
[30] son of Simeon, son of Judah,
son of Joseph, son of Jonam,
son of Eliakim, [31] son of Melea,
son of Menna, son of Mattatha,
son of Nathan, son of David,
[32] son of Jesse, son of Obed,

son of Boaz, son of Salmon,
son of Nahshon, [33] son of Amminadab,
son of Ram, son of Hezron,
son of Perez, son of Judah,
[34] son of Jacob, son of Isaac,
son of Abraham, son of Terah,
son of Nahor, [35] son of Serug,
son of Reu, son of Peleg,
son of Eber, son of Shelah,
[36] son of Cainan, son of Arphaxad,
son of Shem, son of Noah,
son of Lamech, [37] son of Methuselah,
son of Enoch, son of Jared,
son of Mahalalel, son of Cainan,
[38] son of Enos, son of Seth,
son of Adam, son of God.

Genesis 3:15

"I will put hostility between you and the woman,
and between your offspring and her offspring.
He will strike your head,
and you will strike his heel."

Acts 1:6–8

[6] So when they had come together, they asked him, "Lord, are you restoring the kingdom to Israel at this time?"

[7] He said to them, "It is not for you to know times or periods that the Father has set by his own authority. [8] But you will receive power when the Holy Spirit has come on you, and you will be my witnesses in Jerusalem, in all Judea and Samaria, and to the end of the earth."

NOTES

date

Jesus's Early Ministry

THE TEMPTATION OF JESUS

[1] Then Jesus left the Jordan, full of the Holy Spirit, and was led by the Spirit in the wilderness [2] for forty days to be tempted by the devil. He ate nothing during those days, and when they were over, he was hungry. [3] The devil said to him, "If you are the Son of God, tell this stone to become bread."

[4] But Jesus answered him, "It is written: Man must not live on bread alone."

[5] So he took him up and showed him all the kingdoms of the world in a moment of time. [6] The devil said to him, "I will give you their splendor and all this authority, because it has been given over to me, and I can give it to anyone I want. [7] If you, then, will worship me, all will be yours."

[8] And Jesus answered him, "It is written: Worship the Lord your God, and serve him only."

[9] So he took him to Jerusalem, had him stand on the pinnacle of the temple, and said to him, "If you are the Son of God, throw yourself down from here. [10] For it is written:

He will give his angels orders concerning you,
to protect you, [11] and
they will support you with their hands,
so that you will not strike
your foot against a stone."

[12] And Jesus answered him, "It is said: Do not test the Lord your God."

[13] After the devil had finished every temptation, he departed from him for a time.

MINISTRY IN GALILEE

[14] Then Jesus returned to Galilee in the power of the Spirit, and news about him spread throughout the entire vicinity. [15] He was teaching in their synagogues, being praised by everyone.

REJECTION AT NAZARETH

[16] He came to Nazareth, where he had been brought up. As usual, he entered the synagogue on the Sabbath day and stood up to read. [17] The scroll of the prophet Isaiah was given

to him, and unrolling the scroll, he found the place where it was written:

[18] The Spirit of the Lord is on me,
because he has anointed me
to preach good news to the poor.
He has sent me
to proclaim release to the captives
and recovery of sight to the blind,
to set free the oppressed,
[19] to proclaim the year of the Lord's favor.

[20] He then rolled up the scroll, gave it back to the attendant, and sat down. And the eyes of everyone in the synagogue were fixed on him. [21] He began by saying to them, "Today as you listen, this Scripture has been fulfilled."

[22] They were all speaking well of him and were amazed by the gracious words that came from his mouth; yet they said, "Isn't this Joseph's son?"

[23] Then he said to them, "No doubt you will quote this proverb to me: 'Doctor, heal yourself. What we've heard that took place in Capernaum, do here in your hometown also.'"

[24] He also said, "Truly I tell you, no prophet is accepted in his hometown. [25] But I say to you, there were certainly many widows in Israel in Elijah's days, when the sky was shut up for three years and six months while a great famine came over all the land. [26] Yet Elijah was not sent to any of them except a widow at Zarephath in Sidon. [27] And in the prophet Elisha's time, there were many in Israel who had leprosy, and yet not one of them was cleansed except Naaman the Syrian."

[28] When they heard this, everyone in the synagogue was enraged. [29] They got up, drove him out of town, and brought him to the edge of the hill that their town was built on, intending to hurl him over the cliff. [30] But he passed right through the crowd and went on his way.

DRIVING OUT AN UNCLEAN SPIRIT

[31] Then he went down to Capernaum, a town in Galilee, and was teaching them on the Sabbath. [32] They were astonished at his teaching because his message had authority. [33] In the synagogue there was a man with an unclean demonic spirit who cried out with a loud voice, [34] "Leave us alone! What do you have to do with us, Jesus of Nazareth? Have you come to destroy us? I know who you are—the Holy One of God!"

[35] But Jesus rebuked him and said, "Be silent and come out of him!" And throwing him down before them, the demon came out of him without hurting him at all.

[36] Amazement came over them all, and they were saying to one another, "What is this message? For he commands the unclean spirits with authority and power, and they come out!" [37] And news about him began to go out to every place in the vicinity.

HEALINGS AT CAPERNAUM

[38] After he left the synagogue, he entered Simon's house. Simon's mother-in-law was suffering from a high fever, and they asked him about her. [39] So he stood over her and rebuked the fever, and it left her. She got up immediately and began to serve them.

[40] When the sun was setting, all those who had anyone sick with various diseases brought them to him. As he laid his hands on each one of them, he healed them. [41] Also, demons were coming out of many, shouting and saying, "You are the Son of God!" But he rebuked them and would not allow them to speak, because they knew he was the Christ.

[42] When it was day, he went out and made his way to a deserted place. But the crowds were searching for him. They came to him and tried to keep him from leaving them. [43] But he said to them, "It is necessary for me to proclaim the good news about the kingdom of God to the other towns also, because I was sent for this purpose." [44] And he was preaching in the synagogues of Judea.

Deuteronomy 9:6–11

[6] Understand that the LORD your God is not giving you this good land to possess because of your righteousness, for you are a stiff-necked people.

⁷ Remember and do not forget how you provoked the LORD your God in the wilderness. You have been rebelling against the LORD from the day you left the land of Egypt until you reached this place. ⁸ You provoked the LORD at Horeb, and he was angry enough with you to destroy you. ⁹ When I went up the mountain to receive the stone tablets, the tablets of the covenant the LORD made with you, I stayed on the mountain forty days and forty nights. I did not eat food or drink water. ¹⁰ On the day of the assembly the LORD gave me the two stone tablets, inscribed by God's finger. The exact words were on them, which the LORD spoke to you from the fire on the mountain. ¹¹ The LORD gave me the two stone tablets, the tablets of the covenant, at the end of the forty days and forty nights.

¹¹ For he will give his angels orders concerning you,
to protect you in all your ways.
¹² They will support you with their hands
so that you will not strike your foot against a stone.
¹³ You will tread on the lion and the cobra;
you will trample the young lion and the serpent.

¹⁴ Because he has his heart set on me,
I will deliver him;
I will protect him because he knows my name.
¹⁵ When he calls out to me, I will answer him;
I will be with him in trouble.
I will rescue him and give him honor.
¹⁶ I will satisfy him with a long life
and show him my salvation.

Psalm 91

THE PROTECTION OF THE MOST HIGH

¹ The one who lives under the protection of the Most High
dwells in the shadow of the Almighty.

² I will say concerning the LORD, who is my refuge and
my fortress,
my God in whom I trust:
³ He himself will rescue you from the bird trap,
from the destructive plague.
⁴ He will cover you with his feathers;
you will take refuge under his wings.
His faithfulness will be a protective shield.
⁵ You will not fear the terror of the night,
the arrow that flies by day,
⁶ the plague that stalks in darkness,
or the pestilence that ravages at noon.
⁷ Though a thousand fall at your side
and ten thousand at your right hand,
the pestilence will not reach you.
⁸ You will only see it with your eyes
and witness the punishment of the wicked.

⁹ Because you have made the LORD—my refuge,
the Most High—your dwelling place,
¹⁰ no harm will come to you;
no plague will come near your tent.

NOTES

date

The First Disciples

Luke 5

THE FIRST DISCIPLES

[1] As the crowd was pressing in on Jesus to hear God's word, he was standing by Lake Gennesaret. [2] He saw two boats at the edge of the lake; the fishermen had left them and were washing their nets. [3] He got into one of the boats, which belonged to Simon, and asked him to put out a little from the land. Then he sat down and was teaching the crowds from the boat.

[4] When he had finished speaking, he said to Simon, "Put out into deep water and let down your nets for a catch."

[5] "Master," Simon replied, "we've worked hard all night long and caught nothing. But if you say so, I'll let down the nets."

[6] When they did this, they caught a great number of fish, and their nets began to tear. [7] So they signaled to their partners in the other boat to come and help them; they came and filled both boats so full that they began to sink.

[8] When Simon Peter saw this, he fell at Jesus's knees and said, "Go away from me, because I'm a sinful man, Lord!" [9] For he and all those with him were amazed at the catch of fish they had taken, [10] and so were James and John, Zebedee's sons, who were Simon's partners.

"Don't be afraid," Jesus told Simon. "From now on you will be catching people." [11] Then they brought the boats to land, left everything, and followed him.

A MAN CLEANSED

[12] While he was in one of the towns, a man was there who had leprosy all over him. He saw Jesus, fell facedown, and begged him: "Lord, if you are willing, you can make me clean."

[13] Reaching out his hand, Jesus touched him, saying, "I am willing; be made clean," and immediately the leprosy left him. [14] Then he ordered him to tell no one: "But go and show yourself to the priest, and offer what Moses commanded for your cleansing as a testimony to them."

[15] But the news about him spread even more, and large

crowds would come together to hear him and to be healed of their sicknesses. [16] Yet he often withdrew to deserted places and prayed.

THE SON OF MAN FORGIVES AND HEALS

[17] On one of those days while he was teaching, Pharisees and teachers of the law were sitting there who had come from every village of Galilee and Judea, and also from Jerusalem. And the Lord's power to heal was in him. [18] Just then some men came, carrying on a stretcher a man who was paralyzed. They tried to bring him in and set him down before him. [19] Since they could not find a way to bring him in because of the crowd, they went up on the roof and lowered him on the stretcher through the roof tiles into the middle of the crowd before Jesus.

[20] Seeing their faith he said, "Friend, your sins are forgiven."

[21] Then the scribes and the Pharisees began to think to themselves: "Who is this man who speaks blasphemies? Who can forgive sins but God alone?"

[22] But perceiving their thoughts, Jesus replied to them, "Why are you thinking this in your hearts? [23] Which is easier: to say, 'Your sins are forgiven you,' or to say, 'Get up and walk'? [24] But so that you may know that the Son of Man has authority on earth to forgive sins"—he told the paralyzed man, "I tell you: Get up, take your stretcher, and go home."

[25] Immediately he got up before them, picked up what he had been lying on, and went home glorifying God. [26] Then everyone was astounded, and they were giving glory to God. And they were filled with awe and said, "We have seen incredible things today. "

THE CALL OF LEVI

[27] After this, Jesus went out and saw a tax collector named Levi sitting at the tax office, and he said to him, "Follow me." [28] So, leaving everything behind, he got up and began to follow him.

[29] Then Levi hosted a grand banquet for him at his house. Now there was a large crowd of tax collectors and others who were guests with them. [30] But the Pharisees and their scribes were complaining to his disciples, "Why do you eat and drink with tax collectors and sinners?"

[31] Jesus replied to them, "It is not those who are healthy who need a doctor, but those who are sick. [32] I have not come to call the righteous, but sinners to repentance."

A QUESTION ABOUT FASTING

[33] Then they said to him, "John's disciples fast often and say prayers, and those of the Pharisees do the same, but yours eat and drink."

[34] Jesus said to them, "You can't make the wedding guests fast while the groom is with them, can you? [35] But the time will come when the groom will be taken away from them—then they will fast in those days."

[36] He also told them a parable: "No one tears a patch from a new garment and puts it on an old garment. Otherwise, not only will he tear the new, but also the piece from the new garment will not match the old. [37] And no one puts new wine into old wineskins. Otherwise, the new wine will burst the skins, it will spill, and the skins will be ruined. [38] No, new wine is put into fresh wineskins. [39] And no one, after drinking old wine, wants new, because he says, 'The old is better.'"

Isaiah 58:6–12

[6] "Isn't this the fast I choose:
To break the chains of wickedness,
to untie the ropes of the yoke,
to set the oppressed free,
and to tear off every yoke?
[7] Is it not to share your bread with the hungry,
to bring the poor and homeless into your house,
to clothe the naked when you see him,
and not to ignore your own flesh and blood?
[8] Then your light will appear like the dawn,
and your recovery will come quickly.
Your righteousness will go before you,
and the LORD's glory will be your rear guard.

⁹ At that time, when you call, the Lᴏʀᴅ will answer;
when you cry out, he will say, 'Here I am.'
If you get rid of the yoke among you,
the finger-pointing and malicious speaking,
¹⁰ and if you offer yourself to the hungry,
and satisfy the afflicted one,
then your light will shine in the darkness,
and your night will be like noonday.
¹¹ The Lᴏʀᴅ will always lead you,
satisfy you in a parched land,
and strengthen your bones.
You will be like a watered garden
and like a spring whose water never runs dry.
¹² Some of you will rebuild the ancient ruins;
you will restore the foundations laid long ago;
you will be called the repairer of broken walls,
the restorer of streets where people live."

Joel 2:12–17
GOD'S CALL FOR REPENTANCE

¹² Even now—
    this is the Lᴏʀᴅ's declaration—
turn to me with all your heart,
with fasting, weeping, and mourning.
¹³ Tear your hearts,
not just your clothes,
and return to the Lᴏʀᴅ your God.
For he is gracious and compassionate,
slow to anger, abounding in faithful love,
and he relents from sending disaster.
¹⁴ Who knows? He may turn and relent
and leave a blessing behind him,
so you can offer grain and wine
to the Lᴏʀᴅ your God.

¹⁵ Blow the horn in Zion!
Announce a sacred fast;
proclaim an assembly.
¹⁶ Gather the people;
sanctify the congregation;
assemble the aged;
gather the infants,
even babies nursing at the breast.

Let the groom leave his bedroom,
and the bride her honeymoon chamber.
¹⁷ Let the priests, the Lᴏʀᴅ's ministers,
weep between the portico and the altar.
Let them say:
"Have pity on your people, Lᴏʀᴅ,
and do not make your inheritance a disgrace,
an object of scorn among the nations.
Why should it be said among the peoples,
'Where is their God?'"

NOTES   date

He will cover you with his feathers;
you will take refuge under his wings.

Day 6

GRACE DAY

Use this day to pray, rest, and reflect on this week's reading, giving thanks for the grace that is ours in Christ.

² I will say concerning the LORD, who is my refuge and my fortress,
my God in whom I trust:
³ He himself will rescue you from the bird trap,
from the destructive plague.
⁴ He will cover you with his feathers;
you will take refuge under his wings.
His faithfulness will be a protective shield.

Psalm 91:2–4

Day 7

WEEKLY TRUTH

Scripture is God-breathed and true.
When we memorize it, we carry the
gospel with us wherever we go.

This week we will memorize part of
Mary's song of praise in expectation
of giving birth to the Savior.

My soul praises the greatness of the Lord,
and my spirit rejoices in God my Savior...

Luke 1:46b–47

Lord of the Sabbath

Luke 6

LORD OF THE SABBATH

¹ On a Sabbath, he passed through the grainfields. His disciples were picking heads of grain, rubbing them in their hands, and eating them. ² But some of the Pharisees said, "Why are you doing what is not lawful on the Sabbath?"

³ Jesus answered them, "Haven't you read what David and those who were with him did when he was hungry— ⁴ how he entered the house of God and took and ate the bread of the Presence, which is not lawful for any but the priests to eat? He even gave some to those who were with him." ⁵ Then he told them, "The Son of Man is Lord of the Sabbath."

⁶ On another Sabbath he entered the synagogue and was teaching. A man was there whose right hand was shriveled. ⁷ The scribes and Pharisees were watching him closely, to see if he would heal on the Sabbath, so that they could find a charge against him. ⁸ But he knew their thoughts and told the man with the shriveled hand, "Get up and stand here." So he got up and stood there. ⁹ Then Jesus said to them, "I ask you: Is it lawful to do good on the Sabbath or to do evil, to save life or to destroy it?" ¹⁰ After looking around at them all, he told him, "Stretch out your hand." He did, and his hand was restored. ¹¹ They, however, were filled with rage and started discussing with one another what they might do to Jesus.

THE TWELVE APOSTLES

¹² During those days he went out to the mountain to pray and spent all night in prayer to God. ¹³ When daylight came, he summoned his disciples, and he chose twelve of them, whom he also named apostles: ¹⁴ Simon, whom he also named Peter, and Andrew his brother; James and John; Philip and Bartholomew; ¹⁵ Matthew and Thomas; James the son of Alphaeus, and Simon called the Zealot; ¹⁶ Judas the son of James, and Judas Iscariot, who became a traitor.

TEACHING AND HEALING

¹⁷ After coming down with them, he stood on a level place with a large crowd of his disciples and a great number of people from all Judea and Jerusalem and from the seacoast of Tyre

and Sidon. [18] They came to hear him and to be healed of their diseases; and those tormented by unclean spirits were made well. [19] The whole crowd was trying to touch him, because power was coming out from him and healing them all.

THE BEATITUDES

[20] Then looking up at his disciples, he said:

Blessed are you who are poor,
because the kingdom of God is yours.
[21] Blessed are you who are now hungry,
because you will be filled.
Blessed are you who weep now,
because you will laugh.
[22] Blessed are you when people hate you,
when they exclude you, insult you,
and slander your name as evil
because of the Son of Man.

[23] "Rejoice in that day and leap for joy. Take note—your reward is great in heaven, for this is the way their ancestors used to treat the prophets.

WOE TO THE SELF-SATISFIED

[24] But woe to you who are rich,
for you have received your comfort.
[25] Woe to you who are now full,
for you will be hungry.
Woe to you who are now laughing,
for you will mourn and weep.
[26] Woe to you
when all people speak well of you,
for this is the way their ancestors
used to treat the false prophets.

LOVE YOUR ENEMIES

[27] "But I say to you who listen: Love your enemies, do what is good to those who hate you, [28] bless those who curse you, pray for those who mistreat you. [29] If anyone hits you on the cheek, offer the other also. And if anyone takes away your coat, don't hold back your shirt either. [30] Give to everyone who asks you, and from someone who takes your things, don't ask for them back. [31] Just as you want others to do for you, do the same for them. [32] If you love those who love you,

what credit is that to you? Even sinners love those who love them. [33] If you do what is good to those who are good to you, what credit is that to you? Even sinners do that. [34] And if you lend to those from whom you expect to receive, what credit is that to you? Even sinners lend to sinners to be repaid in full. [35] But love your enemies, do what is good, and lend, expecting nothing in return. Then your reward will be great, and you will be children of the Most High. For he is gracious to the ungrateful and evil. [36] Be merciful, just as your Father also is merciful.

DO NOT JUDGE

[37] "Do not judge, and you will not be judged. Do not condemn, and you will not be condemned. Forgive, and you will be forgiven. [38] Give, and it will be given to you; a good measure—pressed down, shaken together, and running over—will be poured into your lap. For with the measure you use, it will be measured back to you."

[39] He also told them a parable: "Can the blind guide the blind? Won't they both fall into a pit? [40] A disciple is not above his teacher, but everyone who is fully trained will be like his teacher.

[41] "Why do you look at the splinter in your brother's eye, but don't notice the beam of wood in your own eye? [42] Or how can you say to your brother, 'Brother, let me take out the splinter that is in your eye,' when you yourself don't see the beam of wood in your eye? Hypocrite! First take the beam of wood out of your eye, and then you will see clearly to take out the splinter in your brother's eye.

A TREE AND ITS FRUIT

[43] "A good tree doesn't produce bad fruit; on the other hand, a bad tree doesn't produce good fruit. [44] For each tree is known by its own fruit. Figs aren't gathered from thornbushes, or grapes picked from a bramble bush. [45] A good person produces good out of the good stored up in his heart. An evil person produces evil out of the evil stored up in his heart, for his mouth speaks from the overflow of the heart.

THE TWO FOUNDATIONS

[46] "Why do you call me 'Lord, Lord,' and don't do the things I say? [47] I will show you what someone is like who comes to

me, hears my words, and acts on them: [48] He is like a man building a house, who dug deep and laid the foundation on the rock. When the flood came, the river crashed against that house and couldn't shake it, because it was well built. [49] But the one who hears and does not act is like a man who built a house on the ground without a foundation. The river crashed against it, and immediately it collapsed. And the destruction of that house was great."

1 Samuel 21:1–6

DAVID FLEES TO NOB

[1] David went to the priest Ahimelech at Nob. Ahimelech was afraid to meet David, so he said to him, "Why are you alone and no one is with you?"

[2] David answered the priest Ahimelech, "The king gave me a mission, but he told me, 'Don't let anyone know anything about the mission I'm sending you on or what I have ordered you to do.' I have stationed my young men at a certain place. [3] Now what do you have on hand? Give me five loaves of bread or whatever can be found."

[4] The priest told him, "There is no ordinary bread on hand. However, there is consecrated bread, but the young men may eat it only if they have kept themselves from women."

[5] David answered him, "I swear that women are being kept from us, as always when I go out to battle. The young men's bodies are consecrated even on an ordinary mission, so of course their bodies are consecrated today." [6] So the priest gave him the consecrated bread, for there was no bread there except the Bread of the Presence that had been removed from the presence of the LORD. When the bread was removed, it had been replaced with warm bread.

James 2:1–7

[1] My brothers and sisters, do not show favoritism as you hold on to the faith in our glorious Lord Jesus Christ. [2] For if someone comes into your meeting wearing a gold ring and dressed in fine clothes, and a poor person dressed in filthy clothes also comes in, [3] if you look with favor on the one wearing the fine clothes and say, "Sit here in a good place," and yet you say to the poor person, "Stand over there," or "Sit here on the floor by my footstool," [4] haven't you made distinctions among yourselves and become judges with evil thoughts?

[5] Listen, my dear brothers and sisters: Didn't God choose the poor in this world to be rich in faith and heirs of the kingdom that he has promised to those who love him? [6] Yet you have dishonored the poor. Don't the rich oppress you and drag you into court? [7] Don't they blaspheme the good name that was invoked over you?

NOTES

date

Much Forgiveness, Much Love

A CENTURION'S FAITH

¹ When he had concluded saying all this to the people who were listening, he entered Capernaum. ² A centurion's servant, who was highly valued by him, was sick and about to die. ³ When the centurion heard about Jesus, he sent some Jewish elders to him, requesting him to come and save the life of his servant. ⁴ When they reached Jesus, they pleaded with him earnestly, saying, "He is worthy for you to grant this, ⁵ because he loves our nation and has built us a synagogue."

⁶ Jesus went with them, and when he was not far from the house, the centurion sent friends to tell him, "Lord, don't trouble yourself, since I am not worthy to have you come under my roof. ⁷ That is why I didn't even consider myself worthy to come to you. But say the word, and my servant will be healed. ⁸ For I too am a man placed under authority, having soldiers under my command. I say to this one, 'Go,' and he goes; and to another, 'Come,' and he comes; and to my servant, 'Do this,' and he does it."

⁹ Jesus heard this and was amazed at him, and turning to the crowd following him, he said, "I tell you, I have not found so great a faith even in Israel." ¹⁰ When those who had been sent returned to the house, they found the servant in good health.

A WIDOW'S SON RAISED TO LIFE

¹¹ Afterward he was on his way to a town called Nain. His disciples and a large crowd were traveling with him. ¹² Just as he neared the gate of the town, a dead man was being carried out. He was his mother's only son, and she was a widow. A large crowd from the city was also with her. ¹³ When the Lord saw her, he had compassion on her and said, "Don't weep." ¹⁴ Then he came up and touched the open coffin, and the pallbearers stopped. And he said, "Young man, I tell you, get up!"

¹⁵ The dead man sat up and began to speak, and Jesus gave him to his mother. ¹⁶ Then fear came over everyone, and they glorified God, saying, "A great prophet has risen among us," and "God has visited his people." ¹⁷ This report about him went throughout Judea and all the vicinity.

IN PRAISE OF JOHN THE BAPTIST

[18] Then John's disciples told him about all these things. So John summoned two of his disciples [19] and sent them to the Lord, asking, "Are you the one who is to come, or should we expect someone else?"

[20] When the men reached him, they said, "John the Baptist sent us to ask you, 'Are you the one who is to come, or should we expect someone else?'"

[21] At that time Jesus healed many people of diseases, afflictions, and evil spirits, and he granted sight to many blind people. [22] He replied to them, "Go and report to John what you have seen and heard: The blind receive their sight, the lame walk, those with leprosy are cleansed, the deaf hear, the dead are raised, and the poor are told the good news, [23] and blessed is the one who isn't offended by me."

[24] After John's messengers left, he began to speak to the crowds about John: "What did you go out into the wilderness to see? A reed swaying in the wind? [25] What then did you go out to see? A man dressed in soft clothes? See, those who are splendidly dressed and live in luxury are in royal palaces. [26] What then did you go out to see? A prophet? Yes, I tell you, and more than a prophet. [27] This is the one about whom it is written:

> See, I am sending my messenger
> ahead of you;
> he will prepare your way before you.

[28] I tell you, among those born of women no one is greater than John, but the least in the kingdom of God is greater than he."

[29] (And when all the people, including the tax collectors, heard this, they acknowledged God's way of righteousness, because they had been baptized with John's baptism. [30] But since the Pharisees and experts in the law had not been baptized by him, they rejected the plan of God for themselves.)

AN UNRESPONSIVE GENERATION

[31] "To what then should I compare the people of this generation, and what are they like? [32] They are like children sitting in the marketplace and calling to each other:

> We played the flute for you,
> but you didn't dance;
> we sang a lament,
> but you didn't weep!

[33] For John the Baptist did not come eating bread or drinking wine, and you say, 'He has a demon!' [34] The Son of Man has come eating and drinking, and you say, 'Look, a glutton and a drunkard, a friend of tax collectors and sinners!' [35] Yet wisdom is vindicated by all her children."

MUCH FORGIVENESS, MUCH LOVE

[36] Then one of the Pharisees invited him to eat with him. He entered the Pharisee's house and reclined at the table. [37] And a woman in the town who was a sinner found out that Jesus was reclining at the table in the Pharisee's house. She brought an alabaster jar of perfume [38] and stood behind him at his feet, weeping, and began to wash his feet with her tears. She wiped his feet with her hair, kissing them and anointing them with the perfume.

[39] When the Pharisee who had invited him saw this, he said to himself, "This man, if he were a prophet, would know who and what kind of woman this is who is touching him—she's a sinner!"

[40] Jesus replied to him, "Simon, I have something to say to you."

He said, "Say it, teacher."

[41] "A creditor had two debtors. One owed five hundred denarii, and the other fifty. [42] Since they could not pay it back, he graciously forgave them both. So, which of them will love him more?"

⁴³ Simon answered, "I suppose the one he forgave more."

"You have judged correctly," he told him. ⁴⁴ Turning to the woman, he said to Simon, "Do you see this woman? I entered your house; you gave me no water for my feet, but she, with her tears, has washed my feet and wiped them with her hair. ⁴⁵ You gave me no kiss, but she hasn't stopped kissing my feet since I came in. ⁴⁶ You didn't anoint my head with olive oil, but she has anointed my feet with perfume. ⁴⁷ Therefore I tell you, her many sins have been forgiven; that's why she loved much. But the one who is forgiven little, loves little." ⁴⁸ Then he said to her, "Your sins are forgiven."

⁴⁹ Those who were at the table with him began to say among themselves, "Who is this man who even forgives sins?"

⁵⁰ And he said to the woman, "Your faith has saved you. Go in peace."

I Kings 17:17–24
THE WIDOW'S SON RAISED

¹⁷ After this, the son of the woman who owned the house became ill. His illness got worse until he stopped breathing. ¹⁸ She said to Elijah, "Man of God, why are you here? Have you come to call attention to my iniquity so that my son is put to death?"

¹⁹ But Elijah said to her, "Give me your son." So he took him from her arms, brought him up to the upstairs room where he was staying, and laid him on his own bed. ²⁰ Then he cried out to the LORD and said, "LORD my God, have you also brought tragedy on the widow I am staying with by killing her son?" ²¹ Then he stretched himself out over the boy three times. He cried out to the LORD and said, "LORD my God, please let this boy's life come into him again!"

²² So the LORD listened to Elijah, and the boy's life came into him again, and he lived. ²³ Then Elijah took the boy, brought him down from the upstairs room into the house, and gave him to his mother. Elijah said, "Look, your son is alive."

²⁴ Then the woman said to Elijah, "Now I know you are a man of God and the LORD's word from your mouth is true."

Psalm 23

THE GOOD SHEPHERD

A psalm of David.

[1] The LORD is my shepherd;
I have what I need.
[2] He lets me lie down in green pastures;
he leads me beside quiet waters.
[3] He renews my life;
he leads me along the right paths
for his name's sake.
[4] Even when I go through the darkest valley,
I fear no danger,
for you are with me;
your rod and your staff—they comfort me.

[5] You prepare a table before me
in the presence of my enemies;
you anoint my head with oil;
my cup overflows.
[6] Only goodness and faithful love will pursue me
all the days of my life,
and I will dwell in the house of the LORD
as long as I live.

NOTES

CHILDREN

THE DEMON-POSSESSED

THE DISREPUTABLE

THE EXCLUDED

GENTILES

THE LOST

Jesus and the

THE POOR

ROMANS

SHEPHERDS

SAMARITANS

THE SICK

THE UNCLEAN

WOMEN

Marginalized

Jesus often ministered to people considered outsiders or outcasts by society, including foreigners, disenfranchised social groups, or those suffering from illness or physical limitation. On the next page are some examples in Luke where Jesus showed special care for the marginalized.

Children

Children were not highly valued for what they could offer or for their faith, yet Jesus cherished them and recognized their humble dependence.

Jesus points to children as models of humility. **9:46–48**

Jesus welcomes children. **18:15–17**

Women

Women did not have the same rights or opportunities as men and were not normally permitted to learn directly from rabbis, but Jesus taught and had great compassion for women.

A group of women help support Jesus and the disciples. **8:1–3**

Mary sits at Jesus's feet as He teaches. **10:38–42**

Women are the first to discover the empty tomb. **24:1–10**

The Demon-Possessed

The demonically possessed were among the outcasts of society, but Jesus healed them and called them to follow Him.

Jesus heals a man possessed by many evil spirits. **8:26–39**

Jesus answers a father's request and casts out a demon from the man's son. **9:37–43**

The Excluded

The weak and powerless were largely ignored, but Jesus said they should be invited in.

Jesus says to show hospitality to those who cannot pay you back. **14:12–14**

The Lost

The lost included all who were morally and spiritually far from God, yet these were the very people Jesus came to seek and save.

Jesus tells parables about how a lost sheep, a lost coin, and a lost son are found and celebrated. **15:1–3**

Jesus initiates friendship with a despised local official. **19:1–10**

Gentiles

Gentiles, or non-Jewish people, were considered unholy and outside of God's saving grace, but Jesus taught that the kingdom of God was for people from every nation.

Jesus is a light for revelation to the Gentiles. **2:32**

All people will see the salvation of God. **3:4–6**

The Poor

Those with little money were looked down upon, but Jesus didn't value people based on their financial resources.

The gospel is good news for the poor. **4:18; 6:20**

The poor will be exalted. **1:51–55; 16:19–31**

Romans

The occupying Roman forces were resented by the Jewish people, yet Jesus was amazed by the faith of a Roman military officer.

Jesus praises a Roman centurion for his faith. **7:1–10**

The Unclean

The unclean, those who violated Jewish purity laws, were stigmatized and isolated from society, but Jesus healed them and restored them to community.

Jesus heals a man with leprosy. **5:12–16**

Jesus heals a bleeding woman. **8:43–48**

Samaritans

The nearby Samaritans were strongly disliked by the Jewish people, but Jesus praised some for acting righteously.

A Samaritan is commended for showing mercy. **10:25–37**

A Samaritan leper returns to thank Jesus for healing him. **17:11–19**

The Sick

The sick were often blamed for their condition, but Jesus healed them and gave them hope.

Jesus heals a paralytic and forgives his sins. **5:17–26**

Jesus heals a man with a shriveled hand on the Sabbath, angering the Jewish religious leaders. **6:6–11**

The Disreputable

The disreputable were shunned because of things they had done, but Jesus freely associated with people others disliked and avoided.

Jesus welcomes tax collectors, who were often regarded as greedy and unscrupulous. **5:27–32**

Jesus forgives a sinful woman because of her faith and praises her for showing Him great love. **7:36–50**

Shepherds

Shepherds were lower-class workers who likely did not observe religious practices, yet God chose to reveal Jesus's birth to them in a spectacular way.

The angel of the Lord announces the birth of Jesus to shepherds in the field keeping watch over their flock. **2:8–20**

Parables and Miracles

Luke 8

MANY WOMEN SUPPORT CHRIST'S WORK

[1] Afterward he was traveling from one town and village to another, preaching and telling the good news of the kingdom of God. The Twelve were with him, [2] and also some women who had been healed of evil spirits and sicknesses: Mary, called Magdalene (seven demons had come out of her); [3] Joanna the wife of Chuza, Herod's steward; Susanna; and many others who were supporting them from their possessions.

THE PARABLE OF THE SOWER

[4] As a large crowd was gathering, and people were coming to Jesus from every town, he said in a parable: [5] "A sower went out to sow his seed. As he sowed, some seed fell along the path; it was trampled on, and the birds of the sky devoured it. [6] Other seed fell on the rock; when it grew up, it withered away, since it lacked moisture. [7] Other seed fell among thorns; the thorns grew up with it and choked it. [8] Still other seed fell on good ground; when it grew up, it produced fruit: a hundred times what was sown." As he said this, he called out, "Let anyone who has ears to hear listen."

WHY JESUS USED PARABLES

[9] Then his disciples asked him, "What does this parable mean?" [10] So he said, "The secrets of the kingdom of God have been given for you to know, but to the rest it is in parables, so that

Looking they may not see,
and hearing they may not understand.

THE PARABLE OF THE SOWER EXPLAINED

[11] "This is the meaning of the parable: The seed is the word of God. [12] The seed along the path are those who have heard and then the devil comes and takes away the word from their hearts, so that they may not believe and be saved. [13] And the seed on the rock are those who, when they hear, receive the word with joy. Having no root, these believe for a while and fall away in a time of testing. [14] As for the seed that fell among thorns, these are the ones who, when they have heard, go on their way and are choked with worries, riches, and pleasures of life, and produce no mature fruit. [15] But the seed in the good ground—these are the ones who, having

heard the word with an honest and good heart, hold on to it and by enduring, produce fruit.

USING YOUR LIGHT

16 "No one, after lighting a lamp, covers it with a basket or puts it under a bed, but puts it on a lampstand so that those who come in may see its light. 17 For nothing is concealed that won't be revealed, and nothing hidden that won't be made known and brought to light. 18 Therefore take care how you listen. For whoever has, more will be given to him; and whoever does not have, even what he thinks he has will be taken away from him."

TRUE RELATIONSHIPS

19 Then his mother and brothers came to him, but they could not meet with him because of the crowd. 20 He was told, "Your mother and your brothers are standing outside, wanting to see you."

21 But he replied to them, "My mother and my brothers are those who hear and do the word of God."

WIND AND WAVE OBEY JESUS

22 One day he and his disciples got into a boat, and he told them, "Let's cross over to the other side of the lake." So they set out, 23 and as they were sailing he fell asleep. Then a fierce windstorm came down on the lake; they were being swamped and were in danger. 24 They came and woke him up, saying, "Master, Master, we're going to die!"

Then he got up and rebuked the wind and the raging waves. So they ceased, and there was a calm. 25 He said to them, "Where is your faith?"

They were fearful and amazed, asking one another, "Who then is this? He commands even the winds and the waves, and they obey him!"

DEMONS DRIVEN OUT BY JESUS

26 Then they sailed to the region of the Gerasenes, which is opposite Galilee. 27 When he got out on land, a demon-possessed man from the town met him. For a long time he had worn no clothes and did not stay in a house but in the tombs. 28 When he saw Jesus, he cried out, fell down before

him, and said in a loud voice, "What do you have to do with me, Jesus, Son of the Most High God? I beg you, don't torment me!" 29 For he had commanded the unclean spirit to come out of the man. Many times it had seized him, and though he was guarded, bound by chains and shackles, he would snap the restraints and be driven by the demon into deserted places.

30 "What is your name?" Jesus asked him.

"Legion," he said, because many demons had entered him. 31 And they begged him not to banish them to the abyss.

32 A large herd of pigs was there, feeding on the hillside. The demons begged him to permit them to enter the pigs, and he gave them permission. 33 The demons came out of the man and entered the pigs, and the herd rushed down the steep bank into the lake and drowned.

34 When the men who tended them saw what had happened, they ran off and reported it in the town and in the countryside. 35 Then people went out to see what had happened. They came to Jesus and found the man the demons had departed from, sitting at Jesus's feet, dressed and in his right mind. And they were afraid. 36 Meanwhile, the eyewitnesses reported to them how the demon-possessed man was delivered. 37 Then all the people of the Gerasene region asked him to leave them, because they were gripped by great fear. So getting into the boat, he returned.

38 The man from whom the demons had departed begged him earnestly to be with him. But he sent him away and said, 39 "Go back to your home, and tell all that God has done for you." And off he went, proclaiming throughout the town how much Jesus had done for him.

A GIRL RESTORED AND A WOMAN HEALED

40 When Jesus returned, the crowd welcomed him, for they were all expecting him. 41 Just then, a man named Jairus came. He was a leader of the synagogue. He fell down at Jesus's feet and pleaded with him to come to his house, 42 because he had an only daughter about twelve years old, and she was dying.

While he was going, the crowds were nearly crushing him. [43] A woman suffering from bleeding for twelve years, who had spent all she had on doctors and yet could not be healed by any, [44] approached from behind and touched the end of his robe. Instantly her bleeding stopped.

[45] "Who touched me?" Jesus asked.

When they all denied it, Peter said, "Master, the crowds are hemming you in and pressing against you."

[46] "Someone did touch me," said Jesus. "I know that power has gone out from me." [47] When the woman saw that she was discovered, she came trembling and fell down before him. In the presence of all the people, she declared the reason she had touched him and how she was instantly healed. [48] "Daughter," he said to her, "your faith has saved you. Go in peace."

[49] While he was still speaking, someone came from the synagogue leader's house and said, "Your daughter is dead. Don't bother the teacher anymore."

[50] When Jesus heard it, he answered him, "Don't be afraid. Only believe, and she will be saved." [51] After he came to the house, he let no one enter with him except Peter, John, James, and the child's father and mother. [52] Everyone was crying and mourning for her. But he said, "Stop crying, because she is not dead but asleep."

[53] They laughed at him, because they knew she was dead. [54] So he took her by the hand and called out, "Child, get up!" [55] Her spirit returned, and she got up at once. Then he gave orders that she be given something to eat. [56] Her parents were astounded, but he instructed them to tell no one what had happened.

Psalm 107:28–32

[28] Then they cried out to the LORD in their trouble,
and he brought them out of their distress.
[29] He stilled the storm to a whisper,
and the waves of the sea were hushed.

[30] They rejoiced when the waves grew quiet.
Then he guided them to the harbor they longed for.
[31] Let them give thanks to the LORD
for his faithful love
and his wondrous works for all humanity.
[32] Let them exalt him in the assembly of the people
and praise him in the council of the elders.

Acts 28:25–28

[25] Disagreeing among themselves, they began to leave after Paul made one statement: "The Holy Spirit was right in saying to your ancestors through the prophet Isaiah [26] when he said,

Go to these people and say:
You will always be listening,
but never understanding;
and you will always be looking,
but never perceiving.
[27] For the hearts of these people
have grown callous,
their ears are hard of hearing,
and they have shut their eyes;
otherwise they might see with their eyes
and hear with their ears,
understand with their heart
and turn,
and I would heal them.

[28] Therefore, let it be known to you that this salvation of God has been sent to the Gentiles; they will listen."

NOTES   *date*

"But you," he asked them, "who do you say that I am?"

Luke 9:20

Day II

TAKE UP YOUR CROSS

Luke 9:1–27

COMMISSIONING THE TWELVE

¹ Summoning the Twelve, he gave them power and authority over all the demons and to heal diseases. ² Then he sent them to proclaim the kingdom of God and to heal the sick.

³ "Take nothing for the road," he told them, "no staff, no traveling bag, no bread, no money; and don't take an extra shirt. ⁴ Whatever house you enter, stay there and leave from there. ⁵ If they do not welcome you, when you leave that town, shake off the dust from your feet as a testimony against them." ⁶ So they went out and traveled from village to village, proclaiming the good news and healing everywhere.

HEROD'S DESIRE TO SEE JESUS

⁷ Herod the tetrarch heard about everything that was going on. He was perplexed, because some said that John had been raised from the dead, ⁸ some that Elijah had appeared, and others that one of the ancient prophets had risen. ⁹ "I beheaded John," Herod said, "but who is this I hear such things about?" And he wanted to see him.

FEEDING OF THE FIVE THOUSAND

¹⁰ When the apostles returned, they reported to Jesus all that they had done. He took them along and withdrew privately to a town called Bethsaida. ¹¹ When the crowds found out, they followed him. He welcomed them, spoke to them about the kingdom of God, and healed those who needed healing.

¹² Late in the day, the Twelve approached and said to him, "Send the crowd away, so that they can go into the surrounding villages and countryside to find food and lodging, because we are in a deserted place here."

¹³ "You give them something to eat," he told them.

"We have no more than five loaves and two fish," they said, "unless we go and buy food for all these people." ¹⁴ (For about five thousand men were there.)

Then he told his disciples, "Have them sit down in groups of about fifty each." ¹⁵ They did what he said, and had them all sit down. ¹⁶ Then he took the five loaves and the two fish, and looking up to heaven, he blessed and broke them. He kept giving them to the disciples to set before the crowd. ¹⁷ Everyone ate and was filled. They picked up twelve baskets of leftover pieces.

PETER'S CONFESSION OF THE MESSIAH

¹⁸ While he was praying in private and his disciples were with him, he asked them, "Who do the crowds say that I am?"

¹⁹ They answered, "John the Baptist; others, Elijah; still others, that one of the ancient prophets has come back."

20 "But you," he asked them, "who do you say that I am?"

Peter answered, "God's Messiah."

HIS DEATH AND RESURRECTION PREDICTED

21 But he strictly warned and instructed them to tell this to no one, 22 saying, "It is necessary that the Son of Man suffer many things and be rejected by the elders, chief priests, and scribes, be killed, and be raised the third day."

TAKE UP YOUR CROSS

23 Then he said to them all, "If anyone wants to follow after me, let him deny himself, take up his cross daily, and follow me. 24 For whoever wants to save his life will lose it, but whoever loses his life because of me will save it. 25 For what does it benefit someone if he gains the whole world, and yet loses or forfeits himself? 26 For whoever is ashamed of me and my words, the Son of Man will be ashamed of him when he comes in his glory and that of the Father and the holy angels. 27 Truly I tell you, there are some standing here who will not taste death until they see the kingdom of God.

Acts 13:44–52

44 The following Sabbath almost the whole town assembled to hear the word of the Lord. 45 But when the Jews saw the crowds, they were filled with jealousy and began to contradict what Paul was saying, insulting him.

46 Paul and Barnabas boldly replied, "It was necessary that the word of God be spoken to you first. Since you reject it and judge yourselves unworthy of eternal life, we are turning to the Gentiles. 47 For this is what the Lord has commanded us:

I have made you
a light for the Gentiles
to bring salvation
to the end of the earth."

48 When the Gentiles heard this, they rejoiced and honored the word of the Lord, and all who had been appointed to eternal life believed. 49 The word of the Lord spread through the whole region. 50 But the Jews incited the prominent God-fearing women and the leading men of the city. They stirred up persecution against Paul and Barnabas and expelled them from their district. 51 But Paul and Barnabas shook the dust off their feet against them and went to Iconium. 52 And the disciples were filled with joy and the Holy Spirit.

Romans 10:1–13

RIGHTEOUSNESS BY FAITH ALONE

1 Brothers and sisters, my heart's desire and prayer to God concerning them is for their salvation. 2 I can testify about them that they have zeal for God, but not according to knowledge. 3 Since they are ignorant of the righteousness of God and attempted to establish their own righteousness, they have not submitted to God's righteousness. 4 For Christ is the end of the law for righteousness to everyone who believes, 5 since Moses writes about the righteousness that is from the law: The one who does these things will live by them. 6 But the righteousness that comes from faith speaks like this: Do not say in your heart, "Who will go up to heaven?" that is, to bring Christ down 7 or, "Who will go down into the abyss?" that is, to bring Christ up from the dead. 8 On the contrary, what does it say? The message is near you, in your mouth and in your heart. This is the message of faith that we proclaim: 9 If you confess with your mouth, "Jesus is Lord," and believe in your heart that God raised him from the dead, you will be saved. 10 One believes with the heart, resulting in righteousness, and one confesses with the mouth, resulting in salvation. 11 For the Scripture says, Everyone who believes on him will not be put to shame, 12 since there is no distinction between Jew and Greek, because the same Lord of all richly blesses all who call on him. 13 For everyone who calls on the name of the Lord will be saved.

We are called to a settled happiness in the Lord whose joy is our strength.

AMY CARMICHAEL

In His Name

Luke 9:28–62

THE TRANSFIGURATION

²⁸ About eight days after this conversation, he took along Peter, John, and James and went up on the mountain to pray. ²⁹ As he was praying, the appearance of his face changed, and his clothes became dazzling white. ³⁰ Suddenly, two men were talking with him—Moses and Elijah. ³¹ They appeared in glory and were speaking of his departure, which he was about to accomplish in Jerusalem.

³² Peter and those with him were in a deep sleep, and when they became fully awake, they saw his glory and the two men who were standing with him. ³³ As the two men were departing from him, Peter said to Jesus, "Master, it's good for us to be here. Let us set up three shelters: one for you, one for Moses, and one for Elijah"—not knowing what he was saying.

³⁴ While he was saying this, a cloud appeared and overshadowed them. They became afraid as they entered the cloud. ³⁵ Then a voice came from the cloud, saying: "This is my Son, the Chosen One; listen to him!"

³⁶ After the voice had spoken, Jesus was found alone. They kept silent, and at that time told no one what they had seen.

THE POWER OF JESUS OVER A DEMON

³⁷ The next day, when they came down from the mountain, a large crowd met him. ³⁸ Just then a man from the crowd cried out, "Teacher, I beg you to look at my son, because he's my only child. ³⁹ A spirit seizes him; suddenly he shrieks, and it throws him into convulsions until he foams at the mouth; severely bruising him, it scarcely ever leaves him. ⁴⁰ I begged your disciples to drive it out, but they couldn't."

⁴¹ Jesus replied, "You unbelieving and perverse generation, how long will I be with you and put up with you? Bring your son here."

⁴² As the boy was still approaching, the demon knocked him down and threw him into severe convulsions. But Jesus rebuked the unclean spirit, healed the boy, and gave him back to his father. ⁴³ And they were all astonished at the greatness of God.

THE SECOND PREDICTION OF HIS DEATH

While everyone was amazed at all the things he was doing, he told his disciples, ⁴⁴ "Let these words sink in: The Son of Man is about to be betrayed into the hands of men."

⁴⁵ But they did not understand this statement; it was concealed from them so that they could not grasp it, and they were afraid to ask him about it.

WHO IS THE GREATEST?

⁴⁶ An argument started among them about who was the greatest of them. ⁴⁷ But Jesus, knowing their inner thoughts, took a little child and had him stand next to him. ⁴⁸ He told them, "Whoever welcomes this little child in my name welcomes me. And whoever welcomes me welcomes him who sent me. For whoever is least among you—this one is great."

IN HIS NAME

⁴⁹ John responded, "Master, we saw someone driving out demons in your name, and we tried to stop him because he does not follow us."

⁵⁰ "Don't stop him," Jesus told him, "because whoever is not against you is for you."

THE JOURNEY TO JERUSALEM

⁵¹ When the days were coming to a close for him to be taken up, he determined to journey to Jerusalem. ⁵² He sent messengers ahead of himself, and on the way they entered a village of the Samaritans to make preparations for him. ⁵³ But they did not welcome him, because he determined to journey to Jerusalem. ⁵⁴ When the disciples James and John saw this, they said, "Lord, do you want us to call down fire from heaven to consume them?"

⁵⁵ But he turned and rebuked them, ⁵⁶ and they went to another village.

FOLLOWING JESUS

⁵⁷ As they were traveling on the road someone said to him, "I will follow you wherever you go."

⁵⁸ Jesus told him, "Foxes have dens, and birds of the sky have nests, but the Son of Man has no place to lay his head."

⁵⁹ Then he said to another, "Follow me."

"Lord," he said, "first let me go bury my father."

⁶⁰ But he told him, "Let the dead bury their own dead, but you go and spread the news of the kingdom of God."

⁶¹ Another said, "I will follow you, Lord, but first let me go and say good-bye to those at my house."

⁶² But Jesus said to him, "No one who puts his hand to the plow and looks back is fit for the kingdom of God."

Exodus 34:29–35

MOSES'S RADIANT FACE

²⁹ As Moses descended from Mount Sinai—with the two tablets of the testimony in his hands as he descended the mountain—he did not realize that the skin of his face shone as a result of his speaking with the LORD. ³⁰ When Aaron and all the Israelites saw Moses, the skin of his face shone! They were afraid to come near him. ³¹ But Moses called out to them, so Aaron and all the leaders of the community returned to him, and Moses spoke to them. ³² Afterward all the Israelites came near, and he commanded them to do everything the LORD had told him on Mount Sinai. ³³ When Moses had finished speaking with them, he put a veil over his face. ³⁴ But whenever Moses went before the LORD to speak with him, he would remove the veil until he came out. After he came out, he would tell the Israelites what he had been commanded, ³⁵ and the Israelites would see that Moses's face was radiant. Then Moses would put the veil over his face again until he went to speak with the LORD.

2 Corinthians 3:18

We all, with unveiled faces, are looking as in a mirror at the glory of the Lord and are being transformed into the same image from glory to glory; this is from the Lord who is the Spirit.

He stilled the storm to a whisper,
and the waves of the sea were hushed.

Day 13

GRACE DAY

Use this day to pray, rest, and reflect on this week's reading, giving thanks for the grace that is ours in Christ.

²⁸ Then they cried out to the LORD in their trouble,
and he brought them out of their distress.
²⁹ He stilled the storm to a whisper,
and the waves of the sea were hushed.
³⁰ They rejoiced when the waves grew quiet.
Then he guided them to the harbor they longed for.
³¹ Let them give thanks to the LORD
for his faithful love
and his wondrous works for all humanity.
³² Let them exalt him in the assembly of the people
and praise him in the council of the elders.

Psalm 107:28–32

Day 14

WEEKLY TRUTH

Scripture is God-breathed and true. When we memorize it, we carry the gospel with us wherever we go.

This week's verse captures the disciples' response to Jesus when He calmed the storm.

They were fearful and amazed, asking one another, "Who then is this? He commands even the winds and the waves, and they obey him!"

Luke 8:25b

The Son Reveals the Father

SENDING OUT THE SEVENTY-TWO

[1] After this, the Lord appointed seventy-two others, and he sent them ahead of him in pairs to every town and place where he himself was about to go. [2] He told them, "The harvest is abundant, but the workers are few. Therefore, pray to the Lord of the harvest to send out workers into his harvest. [3] Now go; I'm sending you out like lambs among wolves. [4] Don't carry a money-bag, traveling bag, or sandals; don't greet anyone along the road. [5] Whatever house you enter, first say, 'Peace to this household.' [6] If a person of peace is there, your peace will rest on him; but if not, it will return to you. [7] Remain in the same house, eating and drinking what they offer, for the worker is worthy of his wages. Don't move from house to house. [8] When you enter any town, and they welcome you, eat the things set before you. [9] Heal the sick who are there, and tell them, 'The kingdom of God has come near you.' [10] When you enter any town, and they don't welcome you, go out into its streets and say, [11] 'We are wiping off even the dust of your town that clings to our feet as a witness against you. Know this for certain: The kingdom of God has come near.' [12] I tell you, on that day it will be more tolerable for Sodom than for that town.

UNREPENTANT TOWNS

[13] "Woe to you, Chorazin! Woe to you, Bethsaida! For if the miracles that were done in you had been done in Tyre and Sidon, they would have repented long ago, sitting in sackcloth and ashes. [14] But it will be more tolerable for Tyre and Sidon at the judgment than for you. [15] And you, Capernaum, will you be exalted to heaven? No, you will go down to Hades. [16] Whoever listens to you listens to me. Whoever rejects you rejects me. And whoever rejects me rejects the one who sent me."

THE RETURN OF THE SEVENTY-TWO

[17] The seventy-two returned with joy, saying, "Lord, even the demons submit to us in your name."

[18] He said to them, "I watched Satan fall from heaven like lightning. [19] Look, I have given you the authority to trample on snakes and scorpions and over all the power of the enemy; nothing at all will harm you. [20] However, don't rejoice that the spirits submit to you, but rejoice that your names are written in heaven."

THE SON REVEALS THE FATHER

[21] At that time he rejoiced in the Holy Spirit and said, "I praise you, Father, Lord of heaven and earth, because you have hidden these things from the wise and intelligent and revealed them to infants. Yes, Father, because this was your good pleasure. [22] All things have been entrusted to me by my Father. No one knows who the Son is except the Father, and who the Father is except the Son, and anyone to whom the Son desires to reveal him."

[23] Then turning to his disciples he said privately, "Blessed are the eyes that see the things you see! [24] For I tell you that many prophets and kings wanted to see the things you see but didn't see them; to hear the things you hear but didn't hear them."

THE PARABLE OF THE GOOD SAMARITAN

[25] Then an expert in the law stood up to test him, saying, "Teacher, what must I do to inherit eternal life?"

[26] "What is written in the law?" he asked him. "How do you read it?"

[27] He answered, "Love the Lord your God with all your heart, with all your soul, with all your strength, and with all your mind," and "your neighbor as yourself."

[28] "You've answered correctly," he told him. "Do this and you will live."

[29] But wanting to justify himself, he asked Jesus, "And who is my neighbor?"

[30] Jesus took up the question and said: "A man was going down from Jerusalem to Jericho and fell into the hands of robbers. They stripped him, beat him up, and fled, leaving him half dead. [31] A priest happened to be going down that road. When he saw him, he passed by on the other side.

³² In the same way, a Levite, when he arrived at the place and saw him, passed by on the other side. ³³ But a Samaritan on his journey came up to him, and when he saw the man, he had compassion. ³⁴ He went over to him and bandaged his wounds, pouring on olive oil and wine. Then he put him on his own animal, brought him to an inn, and took care of him. ³⁵ The next day he took out two denarii, gave them to the innkeeper, and said, 'Take care of him. When I come back I'll reimburse you for whatever extra you spend.'

³⁶ "Which of these three do you think proved to be a neighbor to the man who fell into the hands of the robbers?"

³⁷ "The one who showed mercy to him," he said.

Then Jesus told him, "Go and do the same."

MARTHA AND MARY

³⁸ While they were traveling, he entered a village, and a woman named Martha welcomed him into her home. ³⁹ She had a sister named Mary, who also sat at the Lord's feet and was listening to what he said. ⁴⁰ But Martha was distracted by her many tasks, and she came up and asked, "Lord, don't you care that my sister has left me to serve alone? So tell her to give me a hand."

⁴¹ The Lord answered her, "Martha, Martha, you are worried and upset about many things, ⁴² but one thing is necessary. Mary has made the right choice, and it will not be taken away from her."

Psalm 16
CONFIDENCE IN THE LORD

A Miktam of David.

¹ Protect me, God, for I take refuge in you.
² I said to the LORD, "You are my Lord;
I have nothing good besides you."
³ As for the holy people who are in the land,
they are the noble ones.
All my delight is in them.
⁴ The sorrows of those who take another god
for themselves will multiply;

I will not pour out their drink offerings of blood,
and I will not speak their names with my lips.

⁵ LORD, you are my portion
and my cup of blessing;
you hold my future.
⁶ The boundary lines have fallen for me
in pleasant places;
indeed, I have a beautiful inheritance.

⁷ I will bless the LORD who counsels me—
even at night when my thoughts trouble me.
⁸ I always let the LORD guide me.
Because he is at my right hand,
I will not be shaken.

⁹ Therefore my heart is glad
and my whole being rejoices;
my body also rests securely.
¹⁰ For you will not abandon me to Sheol;
you will not allow your faithful one to see decay.
¹¹ You reveal the path of life to me;
in your presence is abundant joy;
at your right hand are eternal pleasures.

Romans 10:14–17
ISRAEL'S REJECTION OF THE MESSAGE

¹⁴ How, then, can they call on him they have not believed in? And how can they believe without hearing about him? And how can they hear without a preacher? ¹⁵ And how can they preach unless they are sent? As it is written: How beautiful are the feet of those who bring good news. ¹⁶ But not all obeyed the gospel. For Isaiah says, Lord, who has believed our message? ¹⁷ So faith comes from what is heard, and what is heard comes through the message about Christ.

NOTES   *date*

True
Blessedness

Luke 11

THE MODEL PRAYER

[1] He was praying in a certain place, and when he finished, one of his disciples said to him, "Lord, teach us to pray, just as John also taught his disciples."

[2] He said to them, "Whenever you pray, say,

Father,
your name be honored as holy.
Your kingdom come.
[3] Give us each day our daily bread.
[4] And forgive us our sins,
for we ourselves also forgive everyone
in debt to us.
And do not bring us into temptation."

ASK, SEARCH, KNOCK

[5] He also said to them: "Suppose one of you has a friend and goes to him at midnight and says to him, 'Friend, lend me three loaves of bread, [6] because a friend of mine on a journey has come to me, and I don't have anything to offer him.' [7] Then he will answer from inside and say, 'Don't bother me! The door is already locked, and my children and I have gone to bed. I can't get up to give you anything.' [8] I tell you, even though he won't get up and give him anything because he is his friend, yet because of his friend's shameless boldness, he will get up and give him as much as he needs.

[9] "So I say to you, ask, and it will be given to you. Seek, and you will find. Knock, and the door will be opened to you. [10] For everyone who asks receives, and the one who seeks finds, and to the one who knocks, the door will be opened. [11] What father among you, if his son asks for a fish, will give him a snake instead of a fish? [12] Or if he asks for an egg, will give him a scorpion? [13] If you then, who are evil, know how to give good gifts to your children, how much more will the heavenly Father give the Holy Spirit to those who ask him?"

A HOUSE DIVIDED

[14] Now he was driving out a demon that was mute. When the demon came out, the man who had been mute spoke, and the crowds were amazed. [15] But some of them said, "He drives out demons by Beelzebul, the ruler of the demons."

16 And others, as a test, were demanding of him a sign from heaven.

17 Knowing their thoughts, he told them, "Every kingdom divided against itself is headed for destruction, and a house divided against itself falls. 18 If Satan also is divided against himself, how will his kingdom stand? For you say I drive out demons by Beelzebul. 19 And if I drive out demons by Beelzebul, by whom do your sons drive them out? For this reason they will be your judges. 20 If I drive out demons by the finger of God, then the kingdom of God has come upon you. 21 When a strong man, fully armed, guards his estate, his possessions are secure. 22 But when one stronger than he attacks and overpowers him, he takes from him all his weapons he trusted in, and divides up his plunder. 23 Anyone who is not with me is against me, and anyone who does not gather with me scatters.

AN UNCLEAN SPIRIT'S RETURN

24 "When an unclean spirit comes out of a person, it roams through waterless places looking for rest, and not finding rest, it then says, 'I'll go back to my house that I came from.' 25 Returning, it finds the house swept and put in order. 26 Then it goes and brings seven other spirits more evil than itself, and they enter and settle down there. As a result, that person's last condition is worse than the first."

TRUE BLESSEDNESS

27 As he was saying these things, a woman from the crowd raised her voice and said to him, "Blessed is the womb that bore you and the one who nursed you!"

28 He said, "Rather, blessed are those who hear the word of God and keep it."

THE SIGN OF JONAH

29 As the crowds were increasing, he began saying: "This generation is an evil generation. It demands a sign, but no sign will be given to it except the sign of Jonah. 30 For just as Jonah became a sign to the people of Nineveh, so also the Son of Man will be to this generation. 31 The queen of the south will rise up at the judgment with the men of this generation and condemn them, because she came from the ends of the earth to hear the wisdom of Solomon, and look—something

greater than Solomon is here. [32] The men of Nineveh will stand up at the judgment with this generation and condemn it, because they repented at Jonah's preaching, and look—something greater than Jonah is here.

THE LAMP OF THE BODY

[33] "No one lights a lamp and puts it in the cellar or under a basket, but on a lampstand, so that those who come in may see its light. [34] Your eye is the lamp of the body. When your eye is healthy, your whole body is also full of light. But when it is bad, your body is also full of darkness. [35] Take care, then, that the light in you is not darkness. [36] If, therefore, your whole body is full of light, with no part of it in darkness, it will be entirely illuminated, as when a lamp shines its light on you."

RELIGIOUS HYPOCRISY DENOUNCED

[37] As he was speaking, a Pharisee asked him to dine with him. So he went in and reclined at the table. [38] When the Pharisee saw this, he was amazed that he did not first perform the ritual washing before dinner. [39] But the Lord said to him, "Now you Pharisees clean the outside of the cup and dish, but inside you are full of greed and evil. [40] Fools! Didn't he who made the outside make the inside too? [41] But give from what is within to the poor, and then everything is clean for you.

[42] "But woe to you Pharisees! You give a tenth of mint, rue, and every kind of herb, and you bypass justice and love for God. These things you should have done without neglecting the others.

[43] "Woe to you Pharisees! You love the front seat in the synagogues and greetings in the marketplaces.

[44] "Woe to you! You are like unmarked graves; the people who walk over them don't know it."

[45] One of the experts in the law answered him, "Teacher, when you say these things you insult us too."

[46] Then he said: "Woe also to you experts in the law! You load people with burdens that are hard to carry, and yet you yourselves don't touch these burdens with one of your fingers.

[47] "Woe to you! You build tombs for the prophets, and your fathers killed them. [48] Therefore, you are witnesses that you approve the deeds of your fathers, for they killed them, and you build their monuments. [49] Because of this, the wisdom of God said, 'I will send them prophets and apostles, and some of them they will kill and persecute,' [50] so that this generation may be held responsible for the blood of all the prophets shed since the foundation of the world— [51] from the blood of Abel to the blood of Zechariah, who perished between the altar and the sanctuary.

"Yes, I tell you, this generation will be held responsible.

[52] "Woe to you experts in the law! You have taken away the key to knowledge. You didn't go in yourselves, and you hindered those who were trying to go in."

[53] When he left there, the scribes and the Pharisees began to oppose him fiercely and to cross-examine him about many things; [54] they were lying in wait for him to trap him in something he said.

Isaiah 55:6–7

[6] Seek the LORD while he may be found;
call to him while he is near.
[7] Let the wicked one abandon his way
and the sinful one his thoughts;
let him return to the LORD,
so he may have compassion on him,
and to our God, for he will freely forgive.

Romans 8:14–17

[14] For all those led by God's Spirit are God's sons. [15] You did not receive a spirit of slavery to fall back into fear. Instead, you received the Spirit of adoption, by whom we cry out, "Abba, Father!" [16] The Spirit himself testifies together with our spirit that we are God's children, [17] and if children, also heirs—heirs of God and coheirs with Christ—if indeed we suffer with him so that we may also be glorified with him.

date

Acknowledging Christ

BEWARE OF RELIGIOUS HYPOCRISY

1 Meanwhile, a crowd of many thousands came together, so that they were trampling on one another. He began to say to his disciples first, "Be on your guard against the leaven of the Pharisees, which is hypocrisy. 2 There is nothing covered that won't be uncovered, nothing hidden that won't be made known. 3 Therefore, whatever you have said in the dark will be heard in the light, and what you have whispered in an ear in private rooms will be proclaimed on the housetops.

FEAR GOD

4 "I say to you, my friends, don't fear those who kill the body, and after that can do nothing more. 5 But I will show you the one to fear: Fear him who has authority to throw people into hell after death. Yes, I say to you, this is the one to fear! 6 Aren't five sparrows sold for two pennies? Yet not one of them is forgotten in God's sight. 7 Indeed, the hairs of your head are all counted. Don't be afraid; you are worth more than many sparrows.

ACKNOWLEDGING CHRIST

8 "And I say to you, anyone who acknowledges me before others, the Son of Man will also acknowledge him before the angels of God, 9 but whoever denies me before others will be denied before the angels of God. 10 Anyone who speaks a word against the Son of Man will be forgiven, but the one who blasphemes against the Holy Spirit will not be forgiven. 11 Whenever they bring you before synagogues and rulers and authorities, don't worry about how you should defend yourselves or what you should say. 12 For the Holy Spirit will teach you at that very hour what must be said."

THE PARABLE OF THE RICH FOOL

13 Someone from the crowd said to him, "Teacher, tell my brother to divide the inheritance with me."

14 "Friend," he said to him, "who appointed me a judge or arbitrator over you?" 15 He then told them, "Watch out and be on guard against all greed, because one's life is not in the abundance of his possessions."

16 Then he told them a parable: "A rich man's land was very productive. 17 He thought to himself, 'What should I do, since I don't have anywhere to store my crops? 18 I will do this,' he said. 'I'll tear down my barns and build bigger ones and store all my grain and my goods there. 19 Then I'll say to myself, "You have many goods stored up for many years. Take it easy; eat, drink, and enjoy yourself."'

20 "But God said to him, 'You fool! This very night your life is demanded of you. And the things you have prepared—whose will they be?'

21 "That's how it is with the one who stores up treasure for himself and is not rich toward God."

THE CURE FOR ANXIETY

22 Then he said to his disciples: "Therefore I tell you, don't worry about your life, what you will eat; or about the body, what you will wear. 23 For life is more than food and the body more than clothing. 24 Consider the ravens: They don't sow or reap; they don't have a storeroom or a barn; yet God feeds them. Aren't you worth much more than the birds? 25 Can any of you add one moment to his life-span by worrying? 26 If then you're not able to do even a little thing, why worry about the rest?

27 "Consider how the wildflowers grow: They don't labor or spin thread. Yet I tell you, not even Solomon in all his splendor was adorned like one of these. 28 If that's how God clothes the grass, which is in the field today and is thrown into the furnace tomorrow, how much more will he do for you—you of little faith? 29 Don't strive for what you should eat and what you should drink, and don't be anxious. 30 For the Gentile world eagerly seeks all these things, and your Father knows that you need them.

31 "But seek his kingdom, and these things will be provided for you. 32 Don't be afraid, little flock, because your Father delights to give you the kingdom. 33 Sell your possessions and give to the poor. Make money-bags for yourselves that won't grow old, an inexhaustible treasure in heaven, where no thief comes near and no moth destroys. 34 For where your treasure is, there your heart will be also.

[35] "Be ready for service and have your lamps lit. [36] You are to be like people waiting for their master to return from the wedding banquet so that when he comes and knocks, they can open the door for him at once. [37] Blessed will be those servants the master finds alert when he comes. Truly I tell you, he will get ready, have them recline at the table, then come and serve them. [38] If he comes in the middle of the night, or even near dawn, and finds them alert, blessed are those servants. [39] But know this: If the homeowner had known at what hour the thief was coming, he would not have let his house be broken into. [40] You also be ready, because the Son of Man is coming at an hour you do not expect."

REWARDS AND PUNISHMENT

[41] "Lord," Peter asked, "are you telling this parable to us or to everyone?"

[42] The Lord said: "Who then is the faithful and sensible manager his master will put in charge of his household servants to give them their allotted food at the proper time? [43] Blessed is that servant whom the master finds doing his job when he comes. [44] Truly I tell you, he will put him in charge of all his possessions. [45] But if that servant says in his heart, 'My master is delaying his coming,' and starts to beat the male and female servants, and to eat and drink and get drunk, [46] that servant's master will come on a day he does not expect him and at an hour he does not know. He will cut him to pieces and assign him a place with the unfaithful. [47] And that servant who knew his master's will and didn't prepare himself or do it will be severely beaten. [48] But the one who did not know and did what deserved punishment will receive a light beating. From everyone who has been given much, much will be required; and from the one who has been entrusted with much, even more will be expected.

NOT PEACE BUT DIVISION

[49] "I came to bring fire on the earth, and how I wish it were already set ablaze! [50] But I have a baptism to undergo, and how it consumes me until it is finished! [51] Do you think that I came here to bring peace on the earth? No, I tell you, but rather division. [52] From now on, five in one household will be divided: three against two, and two against three.

[53] They will be divided, father against son,
son against father,
mother against daughter,
daughter against mother,
mother-in-law against her daughter-in-law,
and daughter-in-law against mother-in-law."

CONTINUED

WHY ARE THERE FOUR GOSPELS?

A Gospel in the Bible is a book dedicated to telling the story of the life, death, and resurrection of Jesus Christ. Since the early days of Christianity, the Church has recognized four Gospels as giving reliable accounts of the story of Christ: Matthew, Mark, Luke, and John. But why does the Bible include four accounts?

Each Gospel verifies the authenticity of the others. The four writers had a strong connection to Jesus, either as an apostle or as someone close with an apostle. The varied accounts help us see Jesus from different perspectives, giving us a fuller picture than we would get from only one account.

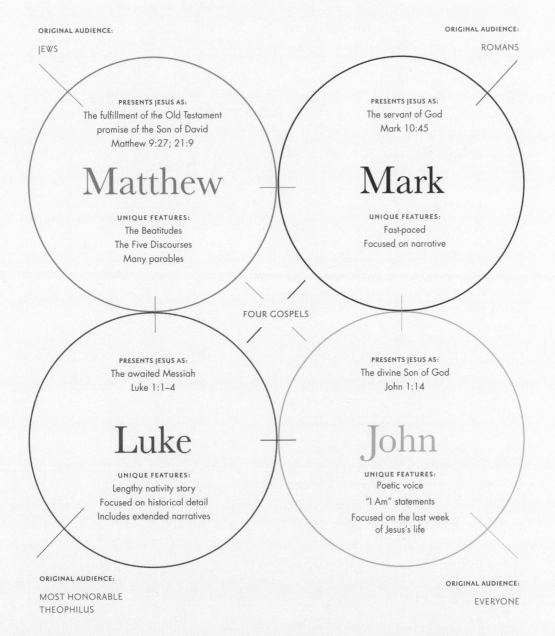

ORIGINAL AUDIENCE:

JEWS

PRESENTS JESUS AS:
The fulfillment of the Old Testament promise of the Son of David
Matthew 9:27; 21:9

Matthew

UNIQUE FEATURES:
The Beatitudes
The Five Discourses
Many parables

ORIGINAL AUDIENCE:

ROMANS

PRESENTS JESUS AS:
The servant of God
Mark 10:45

Mark

UNIQUE FEATURES:
Fast-paced
Focused on narrative

FOUR GOSPELS

PRESENTS JESUS AS:
The awaited Messiah
Luke 1:1–4

Luke

UNIQUE FEATURES:
Lengthy nativity story
Focused on historical detail
Includes extended narratives

PRESENTS JESUS AS:
The divine Son of God
John 1:14

John

UNIQUE FEATURES:
Poetic voice
"I Am" statements
Focused on the last week
of Jesus's life

ORIGINAL AUDIENCE:

MOST HONORABLE
THEOPHILUS

ORIGINAL AUDIENCE:

EVERYONE

INTERPRETING THE TIME

[54] He also said to the crowds: "When you see a cloud rising in the west, right away you say, 'A storm is coming,' and so it does. [55] And when the south wind is blowing, you say, 'It's going to be hot,' and it is. [56] Hypocrites! You know how to interpret the appearance of the earth and the sky, but why don't you know how to interpret this present time?

SETTLING ACCOUNTS

[57] "Why don't you judge for yourselves what is right? [58] As you are going with your adversary to the ruler, make an effort to settle with him on the way. Then he won't drag you before the judge, the judge hand you over to the bailiff, and the bailiff throw you into prison. [59] I tell you, you will never get out of there until you have paid the last cent."

1 Kings 10:4–10

[4] When the queen of Sheba observed all of Solomon's wisdom, the palace he had built, [5] the food at his table, his servants' residence, his attendants' service and their attire, his cupbearers, and the burnt offerings he offered at the LORD's temple, it took her breath away.

[6] She said to the king, "The report I heard in my own country about your words and about your wisdom is true. [7] But I didn't believe the reports until I came and saw with my own eyes. Indeed, I was not even told half. Your wisdom and prosperity far exceed the report I heard. [8] How happy are your men. How happy are these servants of yours, who always stand in your presence hearing your wisdom. [9] Blessed be the LORD your God! He delighted in you and put you on the throne of Israel, because of the LORD's eternal love for Israel. He has made you king to carry out justice and righteousness."

[10] Then she gave the king four and a half tons of gold, a great quantity of spices, and precious stones. Never again did such a quantity of spices arrive as those the queen of Sheba gave to King Solomon.

Psalm 88:1–7
A CRY OF DESPERATION

A song. A psalm of the sons of Korah. For the choir director: according to Mahalath Leannoth. A Maskil of Heman the Ezrahite.

[1] LORD, God of my salvation,
I cry out before you day and night.
[2] May my prayer reach your presence;
listen to my cry.

[3] For I have had enough troubles,
and my life is near Sheol.
[4] I am counted among those going down to the Pit.
I am like a man without strength,
[5] abandoned among the dead.
I am like the slain lying in the grave,
whom you no longer remember,
and who are cut off from your care.

[6] You have put me in the lowest part of the Pit,
in the darkest places, in the depths.
[7] Your wrath weighs heavily on me;
you have overwhelmed me with all your waves.   *Selah*

The basic operating principle of the gospel is "I am accepted by God through the work of Jesus Christ—therefore I obey."

TIMOTHY KELLER

The Narrow Way

Luke 13

REPENT OR PERISH

[1] At that time, some people came and reported to him about the Galileans whose blood Pilate had mixed with their sacrifices. [2] And he responded to them, "Do you think that these Galileans were more sinful than all the other Galileans because they suffered these things? [3] No, I tell you; but unless you repent, you will all perish as well. [4] Or those eighteen that the tower in Siloam fell on and killed—do you think they were more sinful than all the other people who live in Jerusalem? [5] No, I tell you; but unless you repent, you will all perish as well."

THE PARABLE OF THE BARREN FIG TREE

[6] And he told this parable: "A man had a fig tree that was planted in his vineyard. He came looking for fruit on it and found none. [7] He told the vineyard worker, 'Listen, for three years I have come looking for fruit on this fig tree and haven't found any. Cut it down! Why should it even waste the soil?'

[8] "But he replied to him, 'Sir, leave it this year also, until I dig around it and fertilize it. [9] Perhaps it will produce fruit next year, but if not, you can cut it down.'"

HEALING A DAUGHTER OF ABRAHAM

[10] As he was teaching in one of the synagogues on the Sabbath, [11] a woman was there who had been disabled by a spirit for over eighteen years. She was bent over and could not straighten up at all. [12] When Jesus saw her, he called out to her, "Woman, you are free of your disability." [13] Then he laid his hands on her, and instantly she was restored and began to glorify God.

[14] But the leader of the synagogue, indignant because Jesus had healed on the Sabbath, responded by telling the crowd, "There are six days when work should be done; therefore come on those days and be healed and not on the Sabbath day."

¹⁵ But the Lord answered him and said, "Hypocrites! Doesn't each one of you untie his ox or donkey from the feeding trough on the Sabbath and lead it to water? ¹⁶ Satan has bound this woman, a daughter of Abraham, for eighteen years—shouldn't she be untied from this bondage on the Sabbath day?"

¹⁷ When he had said these things, all his adversaries were humiliated, but the whole crowd was rejoicing over all the glorious things he was doing.

THE PARABLES OF THE MUSTARD SEED AND OF THE LEAVEN

¹⁸ He said, therefore, "What is the kingdom of God like, and what can I compare it to? ¹⁹ It's like a mustard seed that a man took and sowed in his garden. It grew and became a tree, and the birds of the sky nested in its branches."

²⁰ Again he said, "What can I compare the kingdom of God to? ²¹ It's like leaven that a woman took and mixed into fifty pounds of flour until all of it was leavened."

THE NARROW WAY

²² He went through one town and village after another, teaching and making his way to Jerusalem. ²³ "Lord," someone asked him, "are only a few people going to be saved?"

He said to them, ²⁴ "Make every effort to enter through the narrow door, because I tell you, many will try to enter and won't be able ²⁵ once the homeowner gets up and shuts the door. Then you will stand outside and knock on the door, saying, 'Lord, open up for us!' He will answer you, 'I don't know you or where you're from.' ²⁶ Then you will say, 'We ate and drank in your presence, and you taught in our streets.' ²⁷ But he will say, 'I tell you, I don't know you or where you're from. Get away from me, all you evildoers!' ²⁸ There will be weeping and gnashing of teeth in that place, when you see Abraham, Isaac, Jacob, and all the prophets in the kingdom of God, but yourselves thrown out. ²⁹ They will come from east and west, from north and south, to share the banquet in the kingdom of God. ³⁰ Note this: Some who are last will be first, and some who are first will be last."

JESUS AND HEROD ANTIPAS

³¹ At that time some Pharisees came and told him, "Go, get out of here. Herod wants to kill you."

³² He said to them, "Go tell that fox, 'Look, I'm driving out demons and performing healings today and tomorrow, and on the third day I will complete my work.' ³³ Yet it is necessary that I travel today, tomorrow, and the next day, because it is not possible for a prophet to perish outside of Jerusalem.

JESUS'S LAMENTATION OVER JERUSALEM

³⁴ "Jerusalem, Jerusalem, who kills the prophets and stones those who are sent to her. How often I wanted to gather your children together, as a hen gathers her chicks under her wings, but you were not willing! ³⁵ See, your house is abandoned to you. I tell you, you will not see me until the time comes when you say, 'Blessed is he who comes in the name of the Lord'!"

Deuteronomy 32:10–14

¹⁰ He found him in a desolate land,
in a barren, howling wilderness;
he surrounded him, cared for him,
and protected him as the pupil of his eye.
¹¹ He watches over his nest like an eagle
and hovers over his young;
he spreads his wings, catches him,
and carries him on his feathers.
¹² The LORD alone led him,
with no help from a foreign god.
¹³ He made him ride on the heights of the land
and eat the produce of the field.
He nourished him with honey from the rock
and oil from flinty rock,
¹⁴ curds from the herd and milk from the flock,
with the fat of lambs,
rams from Bashan, and goats,
with the choicest grains of wheat;
you drank wine from the finest grapes.

LAMENT OF THE EXILES

¹ By the rivers of Babylon—
there we sat down and wept
when we remembered Zion.
² There we hung up our lyres
on the poplar trees,
³ for our captors there asked us for songs,
and our tormentors, for rejoicing:
"Sing us one of the songs of Zion."

⁴ How can we sing the Lᴏʀᴅ's song
on foreign soil?
⁵ If I forget you, Jerusalem,
may my right hand forget its skill.
⁶ May my tongue stick to the roof of my mouth
if I do not remember you,
if I do not exalt Jerusalem as my greatest joy!

⁷ Remember, Lᴏʀᴅ, what the Edomites said
that day at Jerusalem:
"Destroy it! Destroy it
down to its foundations!"
⁸ Daughter Babylon, doomed to destruction,
happy is the one who pays you back
what you have done to us.
⁹ Happy is he who takes your little ones
and dashes them against the rocks.

NOTES

date

"Whoever does not bear his own cross and come after me cannot be my disciple."

Luke 14:27

TEACHINGS ON HUMILITY

Luke 14

A SABBATH CONTROVERSY

[1] One Sabbath, when he went in to eat at the house of one of the leading Pharisees, they were watching him closely. [2] There in front of him was a man whose body was swollen with fluid. [3] In response, Jesus asked the law experts and the Pharisees, "Is it lawful to heal on the Sabbath or not?" [4] But they kept silent. He took the man, healed him, and sent him away. [5] And to them, he said, "Which of you whose son or ox falls into a well, will not immediately pull him out on the Sabbath day?" [6] They could find no answer to these things.

TEACHINGS ON HUMILITY

[7] He told a parable to those who were invited, when he noticed how they would choose the best places for themselves: [8] "When you are invited by someone to a wedding banquet, don't recline at the best place, because a more distinguished person than you may have been invited by your host. [9] The one who invited both of you may come and say to you, 'Give your place to this man,' and then in humiliation, you will proceed to take the lowest place.

[10] "But when you are invited, go and recline in the lowest place, so that when the one who invited you comes, he will say to you, 'Friend, move up higher.' You will then be honored in the presence of all the other guests. [11] For everyone who exalts himself will be humbled, and the one who humbles himself will be exalted."

[12] He also said to the one who had invited him, "When you give a lunch or a dinner, don't invite your friends, your brothers or sisters, your relatives, or your rich neighbors, because they might invite you back, and you would be repaid. [13] On the contrary, when you host a banquet, invite those who are poor, maimed, lame, or blind. [14] And you will be blessed, because they cannot repay you; for you will be repaid at the resurrection of the righteous."

THE PARABLE OF THE LARGE BANQUET

[15] When one of those who reclined at the table with him heard these things, he said to him, "Blessed is the one who will eat bread in the kingdom of God!"

[16] Then he told him: "A man was giving a large banquet and invited many. [17] At the time of the banquet, he sent his servant to tell those who were invited, 'Come, because everything is now ready.'

[18] "But without exception they all began to make excuses. The first one said to him, 'I have bought a field, and I must go out and see it. I ask you to excuse me.'

¹⁹ "Another said, 'I have bought five yoke of oxen, and I'm going to try them out. I ask you to excuse me.'

²⁰ "And another said, 'I just got married, and therefore I'm unable to come.'

²¹ "So the servant came back and reported these things to his master. Then in anger, the master of the house told his servant, 'Go out quickly into the streets and alleys of the city, and bring in here the poor, maimed, blind, and lame.'

²² "'Master,' the servant said, 'what you ordered has been done, and there's still room.'

²³ "Then the master told the servant, 'Go out into the highways and hedges and make them come in, so that my house may be filled. ²⁴ For I tell you, not one of those people who were invited will enjoy my banquet.'"

THE COST OF FOLLOWING JESUS

²⁵ Now great crowds were traveling with him. So he turned and said to them: ²⁶ "If anyone comes to me and does not hate his own father and mother, wife and children, brothers and sisters—yes, and even his own life—he cannot be my disciple. ²⁷ Whoever does not bear his own cross and come after me cannot be my disciple.

²⁸ "For which of you, wanting to build a tower, doesn't first sit down and calculate the cost to see if he has enough to complete it? ²⁹ Otherwise, after he has laid the foundation and cannot finish it, all the onlookers will begin to ridicule him, ³⁰ saying, 'This man started to build and wasn't able to finish.'

³¹ "Or what king, going to war against another king, will not first sit down and decide if he is able with ten thousand to oppose the one who comes against him with twenty thousand? ³² If not, while the other is still far off, he sends a delegation and asks for terms of peace. ³³ In the same way, therefore, every one of you who does not renounce all his possessions cannot be my disciple.

³⁴ "Now, salt is good, but if salt should lose its taste, how will it be made salty? ³⁵ It isn't fit for the soil or for the manure pile; they throw it out. Let anyone who has ears to hear listen."

Proverbs 25:6–7

⁶ Don't boast about yourself before the king,
and don't stand in the place of the great;
⁷ for it is better for him to say to you, "Come up here!"
than to demote you in plain view of a noble.

Romans 12:16

Live in harmony with one another. Do not be proud; instead, associate with the humble. Do not be wise in your own estimation.

How beautiful are the feet of those who bring good news.

Day 20

GRACE DAY

Use this day to pray, rest, and reflect on this week's reading, giving thanks for the grace that is ours in Christ.

[14] How, then, can they call on him they have not believed in? And how can they believe without hearing about him? And how can they hear without a preacher? [15] And how can they preach unless they are sent? As it is written: How beautiful are the feet of those who bring good news. [16] But not all obeyed the gospel. For Isaiah says, Lord, who has believed our message? [17] So faith comes from what is heard, and what is heard comes through the message about Christ.

Romans 10:14–17

WEEKLY TRUTH

Scripture is God-breathed and true. When we memorize it, we carry the gospel with us wherever we go.

This week we will memorize a verse about the relationship between God and His people.

"Don't be afraid, little flock, because your Father delights to give you the kingdom."

Luke 12:32

Rejoice with me, because I have found my lost sheep!

Luke 15:6

LOST AND FOUND

Luke 15

THE PARABLE OF THE LOST SHEEP

[1] All the tax collectors and sinners were approaching to listen to him. [2] And the Pharisees and scribes were complaining, "This man welcomes sinners and eats with them."

[3] So he told them this parable: [4] "What man among you, who has a hundred sheep and loses one of them, does not leave the ninety-nine in the open field and go after the lost one until he finds it? [5] When he has found it, he joyfully puts it on his shoulders, [6] and coming home, he calls his friends and neighbors together, saying to them, 'Rejoice with me, because I have found my lost sheep!' [7] I tell you, in the same way, there will be more joy in heaven over one sinner who repents than over ninety-nine righteous people who don't need repentance.

THE PARABLE OF THE LOST COIN

[8] "Or what woman who has ten silver coins, if she loses one coin, does not light a lamp, sweep the house, and search carefully until she finds it? [9] When she finds it, she calls her friends and neighbors together, saying, 'Rejoice with me, because I have found the silver coin I lost!' [10] I tell you, in the same way, there is joy in the presence of God's angels over one sinner who repents."

THE PARABLE OF THE LOST SON

[11] He also said: "A man had two sons. [12] The younger of them said to his father, 'Father, give me the share of the estate I have coming to me.' So he distributed the assets to them. [13] Not many days later, the younger son gathered together all he had and traveled to a distant country, where he squandered his estate in foolish living. [14] After he had spent everything, a severe famine struck that country, and he had nothing. [15] Then he went to work for one of the citizens of that country, who sent him into his fields to feed pigs. [16] He longed to eat his fill from the pods that the pigs were eating, but no one would give him anything. [17] When he came to his senses, he said, 'How many of my father's hired workers have more than enough food, and here I am dying of hunger! [18] I'll get up, go to my father, and say to him, "Father, I have sinned against heaven and in your sight. [19] I'm no longer worthy to be called your son. Make me like one of your hired workers."' [20] So he got up and went to his father. But while the son was still a long way off, his father saw him and was filled with compassion. He ran, threw his arms around his neck, and kissed him. [21] The son said to him, 'Father, I have sinned against heaven and in your sight. I'm no longer worthy to be called your son.'

22 "But the father told his servants, 'Quick! Bring out the best robe and put it on him; put a ring on his finger and sandals on his feet. 23 Then bring the fattened calf and slaughter it, and let's celebrate with a feast, 24 because this son of mine was dead and is alive again; he was lost and is found!' So they began to celebrate.

25 "Now his older son was in the field; as he came near the house, he heard music and dancing. 26 So he summoned one of the servants, questioning what these things meant. 27 'Your brother is here,' he told him, 'and your father has slaughtered the fattened calf because he has him back safe and sound.'

28 "Then he became angry and didn't want to go in. So his father came out and pleaded with him. 29 But he replied to his father, 'Look, I have been slaving many years for you, and I have never disobeyed your orders, yet you never gave me a goat so that I could celebrate with my friends. 30 But when this son of yours came, who has devoured your assets with prostitutes, you slaughtered the fattened calf for him.'

31 "'Son,' he said to him, 'you are always with me, and everything I have is yours. 32 But we had to celebrate and rejoice, because this brother of yours was dead and is alive again; he was lost and is found.'"

Ezekiel 34:11–12

11 "For this is what the Lord God says: See, I myself will search for my flock and look for them. 12 As a shepherd looks for his sheep on the day he is among his scattered flock, so I will look for my flock. I will rescue them from all the places where they have been scattered on a day of clouds and total darkness."

Romans 3:9–20

THE WHOLE WORLD GUILTY BEFORE GOD

9 What then? Are we any better off? Not at all! For we have already charged that both Jews and Gentiles are all under sin, 10 as it is written:

There is no one righteous, not even one.
11 There is no one who understands;
there is no one who seeks God.
12 All have turned away;
all alike have become worthless.
There is no one who does what is good,
not even one.
13 Their throat is an open grave;
they deceive with their tongues.
Vipers' venom is under their lips.
14 Their mouth is full of cursing and bitterness.
15 Their feet are swift to shed blood;
16 ruin and wretchedness are in their paths,
17 and the path of peace they have not known.
18 There is no fear of God before their eyes.

19 Now we know that whatever the law says, it speaks to those who are subject to the law, so that every mouth may be shut and the whole world may become subject to God's judgment. 20 For no one will be justified in his sight by the works of the law, because the knowledge of sin comes through the law.

NOTES

date

Kingdom Values

THE PARABLE OF THE DISHONEST MANAGER

¹ Now he said to the disciples: "There was a rich man who received an accusation that his manager was squandering his possessions. ² So he called the manager in and asked, 'What is this I hear about you? Give an account of your management, because you can no longer be my manager.'

³ "Then the manager said to himself, 'What will I do since my master is taking the management away from me? I'm not strong enough to dig; I'm ashamed to beg. ⁴ I know what I'll do so that when I'm removed from management, people will welcome me into their homes.'

⁵ "So he summoned each one of his master's debtors. 'How much do you owe my master?' he asked the first one.

⁶ "'A hundred measures of olive oil,' he said.

"'Take your invoice,' he told him, 'sit down quickly, and write fifty.'

⁷ "Next he asked another, 'How much do you owe?'

"'A hundred measures of wheat,' he said.

"'Take your invoice,' he told him, 'and write eighty.'

⁸ "The master praised the unrighteous manager because he had acted shrewdly. For the children of this age are more shrewd than the children of light in dealing with their own people. ⁹ And I tell you, make friends for yourselves by means of worldly wealth so that when it fails, they may welcome you into eternal dwellings. ¹⁰ Whoever is faithful in very little is also faithful in much, and whoever is unrighteous in very little is also unrighteous in much. ¹¹ So if you have not been faithful with worldly wealth, who will trust you with what is genuine? ¹² And if you have not been faithful with what belongs to someone else, who will give you what is your own? ¹³ No servant can serve two masters, since either he will hate one and love the other, or he will be devoted to one and despise the other. You cannot serve both God and money."

KINGDOM VALUES

¹⁴ The Pharisees, who were lovers of money, were listening to all these things and scoffing at him. ¹⁵ And he told them, "You are the ones who justify yourselves in the sight of others, but God knows your hearts. For what is highly admired by people is revolting in God's sight.

¹⁶ "The Law and the Prophets were until John; since then, the good news of the kingdom of God has been proclaimed, and everyone is urgently invited to enter it. ¹⁷ But it is easier for heaven and earth to pass away than for one stroke of a letter in the law to drop out.

¹⁸ "Everyone who divorces his wife and marries another woman commits adultery, and everyone who marries a woman divorced from her husband commits adultery.

THE RICH MAN AND LAZARUS

¹⁹ "There was a rich man who would dress in purple and fine linen, feasting lavishly every day. ²⁰ But a poor man named Lazarus, covered with sores, was lying at his gate. ²¹ He longed to be filled with what fell from the rich man's table, but instead the dogs would come and lick his sores. ²² One day the poor man died and was carried away by the angels to Abraham's side. The rich man also died and was buried. ²³ And being in torment in Hades, he looked up and saw Abraham a long way off, with Lazarus at his side. ²⁴ 'Father Abraham!' he called out, 'Have mercy on me and send Lazarus to dip the tip of his finger in water and cool my tongue, because I am in agony in this flame!'

²⁵ "'Son,' Abraham said, 'remember that during your life you received your good things, just as Lazarus received bad things, but now he is comforted here, while you are in agony. ²⁶ Besides all this, a great chasm has been fixed between us and you, so that those who want to pass over from here to you cannot; neither can those from there cross over to us.'

²⁷ "'Father,' he said, 'then I beg you to send him to my father's house— ²⁸ because I have five brothers—to warn them, so they won't also come to this place of torment.'

²⁹ "But Abraham said, 'They have Moses and the prophets; they should listen to them.'

³⁰ "'No, father Abraham,' he said. 'But if someone from the dead goes to them, they will repent.'

³¹ "But he told him, 'If they don't listen to Moses and the prophets, they will not be persuaded if someone rises from the dead.'"

Proverbs 15:16

Better a little with the fear of the Lord
than great treasure with turmoil.

1 Corinthians 4:7–13

⁷ For who makes you so superior? What do you have that you didn't receive? If, in fact, you did receive it, why do you boast as if you hadn't received it? ⁸ You are already full! You are already rich! You have begun to reign as kings without us—and I wish you did reign, so that we could also reign with you! ⁹ For I think God has displayed us, the apostles, in last place, like men condemned to die: We have become a spectacle to the world, both to angels and to people. ¹⁰ We are fools for Christ, but you are wise in Christ! We are weak, but you are strong! You are distinguished, but we are dishonored! ¹¹ Up to the present hour we are both hungry and thirsty; we are poorly clothed, roughly treated, homeless; ¹² we labor, working with our own hands. When we are reviled, we bless; when we are persecuted, we endure it; ¹³ when we are slandered, we respond graciously. Even now, we are like the scum of the earth, like everyone's garbage.

NOTES   *date*

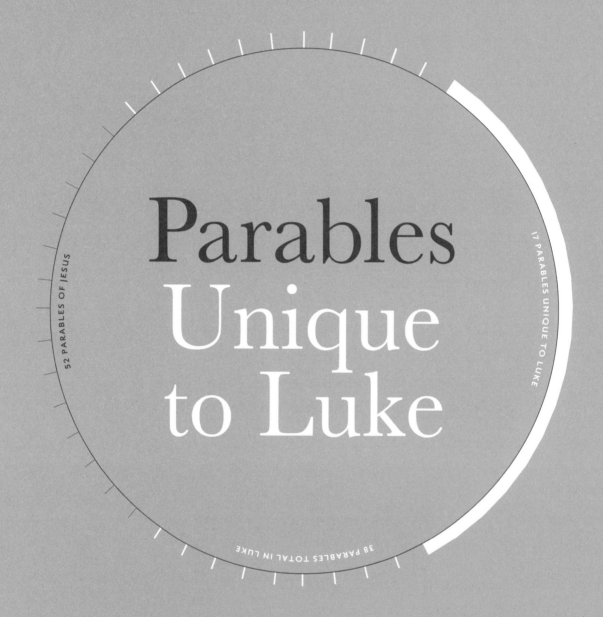

Parables Unique to Luke

52 PARABLES OF JESUS

38 PARABLES TOTAL IN LUKE

17 PARABLES UNIQUE TO LUKE

Jesus often spoke in parables. Told to illustrate truth, prompt questions, and punctuate important teachings, parables are stories that were used to address something happening in the moment or to correct a common religious misconception. Jesus also used parables to describe Himself or the kingdom of God. Listed to the right are the parables unique to Luke's Gospel.

The two debtors
7:41–43

The good Samaritan
10:30–37

The friend at midnight
11:5–8

The rich fool
12:16–21

Slaves waiting for their master's return
12:35–38

The barren fig tree
13:6–9

The wedding feast
14:7–11

Building a tower
14:28–30

Waging war
14:31–32

The lost coin
15:8–10

The lost son
15:11–32

The dishonest manager
16:1–13

The rich man and Lazarus
16:19–31

The servant's responsibilities
17:5–10

The persistent widow
18:1–8

The Pharisee and the tax collector
18:9–14

The ten minas
19:11–27

Faith and Duty

Luke 17

WARNINGS FROM JESUS

[1] He said to his disciples, "Offenses will certainly come, but woe to the one through whom they come! [2] It would be better for him if a millstone were hung around his neck and he were thrown into the sea than for him to cause one of these little ones to stumble. [3] Be on your guard. If your brother sins, rebuke him, and if he repents, forgive him. [4] And if he sins against you seven times in a day, and comes back to you seven times, saying, 'I repent,' you must forgive him."

FAITH AND DUTY

[5] The apostles said to the Lord, "Increase our faith."

[6] "If you have faith the size of a mustard seed," the Lord said, "you can say to this mulberry tree, 'Be uprooted and planted in the sea,' and it will obey you.

[7] "Which one of you having a servant tending sheep or plowing will say to him when he comes in from the field, 'Come at once and sit down to eat'? [8] Instead, will he not tell him, 'Prepare something for me to eat, get ready, and serve me while I eat and drink; later you can eat and drink'? [9] Does he thank that servant because he did what was commanded? [10] In the same way, when you have done all that you were commanded, you should say, 'We are worthless servants; we've only done our duty.'"

TEN MEN HEALED

[11] While traveling to Jerusalem, he passed between Samaria and Galilee. [12] As he entered a village, ten men with leprosy met him. They stood at a distance [13] and raised their voices, saying, "Jesus, Master, have mercy on us!"

[14] When he saw them, he told them, "Go and show yourselves to the priests." And while they were going, they were cleansed.

[15] But one of them, seeing that he was healed, returned and, with a loud voice, gave glory to God. [16] He fell facedown at his feet, thanking him. And he was a Samaritan.

¹⁷ Then Jesus said, "Were not ten cleansed? Where are the nine? ¹⁸ Didn't any return to give glory to God except this foreigner?" ¹⁹ And he told him, "Get up and go on your way. Your faith has saved you."

THE COMING OF THE KINGDOM

²⁰ Being asked by the Pharisees when the kingdom of God would come, he answered them, "The kingdom of God is not coming with something observable; ²¹ no one will say, 'See here!' or 'There!' For you see, the kingdom of God is in your midst."

²² Then he told the disciples: "The days are coming when you will long to see one of the days of the Son of Man, but you won't see it. ²³ They will say to you, 'See there!' or 'See here!' Don't follow or run after them. ²⁴ For as the lightning flashes from horizon to horizon and lights up the sky, so the Son of Man will be in his day. ²⁵ But first it is necessary that he suffer many things and be rejected by this generation.

²⁶ "Just as it was in the days of Noah, so it will be in the days of the Son of Man: ²⁷ People went on eating, drinking, marrying and giving in marriage until the day Noah boarded the ark, and the flood came and destroyed them all. ²⁸ It will be the same as it was in the days of Lot: People went on eating, drinking, buying, selling, planting, building. ²⁹ But on the day Lot left Sodom, fire and sulfur rained from heaven and destroyed them all. ³⁰ It will be like that on the day the Son of Man is revealed. ³¹ On that day, a man on the housetop, whose belongings are in the house, must not come down to get them. Likewise the man who is in the field must not turn back. ³² Remember Lot's wife! ³³ Whoever tries to make his life secure will lose it, and whoever loses his life will preserve it. ³⁴ I tell you, on that night two will be in one bed; one will be taken and the other will be left. ³⁵ Two women will be grinding grain together; one will be taken and the other left."

³⁷ "Where, Lord?" they asked him.

He said to them, "Where the corpse is, there also the vultures will be gathered."

Deuteronomy 10:12–13

WHAT GOD REQUIRES

[12] And now, Israel, what does the LORD your God ask of you except to fear the LORD your God by walking in all his ways, to love him, and to worship the LORD your God with all your heart and all your soul? [13] Keep the LORD's commands and statutes I am giving you today, for your own good.

Hebrews 3:7–11

WARNING AGAINST UNBELIEF

[7] Therefore, as the Holy Spirit says:

Today, if you hear his voice,
[8] do not harden your hearts as in the rebellion,
on the day of testing in the wilderness,
[9] where your fathers tested me, tried me,
and saw my works [10] for forty years.
Therefore I was provoked to anger with that generation
and said, "They always go astray in their hearts,
and they have not known my ways."
[11] So I swore in my anger,
"They will not enter my rest."

NOTES

"Nevertheless, when the Son of Man comes, will he find faith on earth?"

Luke 18:8

ENTERING THE KINGDOM

Luke 18

THE PARABLE OF THE PERSISTENT WIDOW

¹ Now he told them a parable on the need for them to pray always and not give up. ² "There was a judge in a certain town who didn't fear God or respect people. ³ And a widow in that town kept coming to him, saying, 'Give me justice against my adversary.'

⁴ "For a while he was unwilling, but later he said to himself, 'Even though I don't fear God or respect people, ⁵ yet because this widow keeps pestering me, I will give her justice, so that she doesn't wear me out by her persistent coming.'"

⁶ Then the Lord said, "Listen to what the unjust judge says. ⁷ Will not God grant justice to his elect who cry out to him day and night? Will he delay helping them? ⁸ I tell you that he will swiftly grant them justice. Nevertheless, when the Son of Man comes, will he find faith on earth?"

THE PARABLE OF THE PHARISEE AND THE TAX COLLECTOR

⁹ He also told this parable to some who trusted in themselves that they were righteous and looked down on everyone else: ¹⁰ "Two men went up to the temple to pray, one a Pharisee and the other a tax collector. ¹¹ The Pharisee was standing and praying like this about himself: 'God, I thank you that I'm not like other people—greedy, unrighteous, adulterers, or even like this tax collector. ¹² I fast twice a week; I give a tenth of everything I get.'

¹³ "But the tax collector, standing far off, would not even raise his eyes to heaven but kept striking his chest and saying, 'God, have mercy on me, a sinner!' ¹⁴ I tell you, this one went down to his house justified rather than the other; because everyone who exalts himself will be humbled, but the one who humbles himself will be exalted."

BLESSING THE CHILDREN

¹⁵ People were bringing infants to him so he might touch them, but when the disciples saw it, they rebuked them. ¹⁶ Jesus, however, invited them: "Let the little children come to me, and don't stop them, because the kingdom of God belongs to such as these. ¹⁷ Truly I tell you, whoever does not receive the kingdom of God like a little child will never enter it."

THE RICH YOUNG RULER

¹⁸ A ruler asked him, "Good teacher, what must I do to inherit eternal life?"

¹⁹ "Why do you call me good?" Jesus asked him. "No one is

good except God alone. ²⁰ You know the commandments: Do not commit adultery; do not murder; do not steal; do not bear false witness; honor your father and mother."

²¹ "I have kept all these from my youth," he said.

²² When Jesus heard this, he told him, "You still lack one thing: Sell all you have and distribute it to the poor, and you will have treasure in heaven. Then come, follow me."

²³ After he heard this, he became extremely sad, because he was very rich.

POSSESSIONS AND THE KINGDOM

²⁴ Seeing that he became sad, Jesus said, "How hard it is for those who have wealth to enter the kingdom of God! ²⁵ For it is easier for a camel to go through the eye of a needle than for a rich person to enter the kingdom of God."

²⁶ Those who heard this asked, "Then who can be saved?"

²⁷ He replied, "What is impossible with man is possible with God."

²⁸ Then Peter said, "Look, we have left what we had and followed you."

²⁹ So he said to them, "Truly I tell you, there is no one who has left a house, wife or brothers or sisters, parents or children because of the kingdom of God, ³⁰ who will not receive many times more at this time, and eternal life in the age to come."

THE THIRD PREDICTION OF HIS DEATH

³¹ Then he took the Twelve aside and told them, "See, we are going up to Jerusalem. Everything that is written through the prophets about the Son of Man will be accomplished. ³² For he will be handed over to the Gentiles, and he will be mocked, insulted, spit on; ³³ and after they flog him, they will kill him, and he will rise on the third day."

³⁴ They understood none of these things. The meaning of the saying was hidden from them, and they did not grasp what was said.

A BLIND MAN RECEIVES HIS SIGHT

³⁵ As he approached Jericho, a blind man was sitting by the road begging. ³⁶ Hearing a crowd passing by, he inquired what was happening. ³⁷ "Jesus of Nazareth is passing by," they told him.

³⁸ So he called out, "Jesus, Son of David, have mercy on me!" ³⁹ Then those in front told him to keep quiet, but he kept crying out all the more, "Son of David, have mercy on me!"

⁴⁰ Jesus stopped and commanded that he be brought to him. When he came closer, he asked him, ⁴¹ "What do you want me to do for you?"

"Lord," he said, "I want to see."

⁴² "Receive your sight." Jesus told him. "Your faith has saved you." ⁴³ Instantly he could see, and he began to follow him, glorifying God. All the people, when they saw it, gave praise to God.

Genesis 18:13–15

¹³ But the LORD asked Abraham, "Why did Sarah laugh, saying, 'Can I really have a baby when I'm old?' ¹⁴ Is anything impossible for the LORD? At the appointed time I will come back to you, and in about a year she will have a son."

¹⁵ Sarah denied it. "I did not laugh," she said, because she was afraid.

But he replied, "No, you did laugh."

Jeremiah 32:17

Oh, Lord GOD! You yourself made the heavens and earth by your great power and with your outstretched arm. Nothing is too difficult for you!

NOTES

date

The Triumphal Entry

JESUS VISITS ZACCHAEUS

¹ He entered Jericho and was passing through. ² There was a man named Zacchaeus who was a chief tax collector, and he was rich. ³ He was trying to see who Jesus was, but he was not able because of the crowd, since he was a short man. ⁴ So running ahead, he climbed up a sycamore tree to see Jesus, since he was about to pass that way. ⁵ When Jesus came to the place, he looked up and said to him, "Zacchaeus, hurry and come down because today it is necessary for me to stay at your house."

⁶ So he quickly came down and welcomed him joyfully. ⁷ All who saw it began to complain, "He's gone to stay with a sinful man."

⁸ But Zacchaeus stood there and said to the Lord, "Look, I'll give half of my possessions to the poor, Lord. And if I have extorted anything from anyone, I'll pay back four times as much."

⁹ "Today salvation has come to this house," Jesus told him, "because he too is a son of Abraham. ¹⁰ For the Son of Man has come to seek and to save the lost."

THE PARABLE OF THE TEN MINAS

¹¹ As they were listening to this, he went on to tell a parable because he was near Jerusalem, and they thought the kingdom of God was going to appear right away.

¹² Therefore he said: "A nobleman traveled to a far country to receive for himself authority to be king and then to return. ¹³ He called ten of his servants, gave them ten minas, and told them, 'Engage in business until I come back.'

¹⁴ "But his subjects hated him and sent a delegation after him, saying, 'We don't want this man to rule over us.'

¹⁵ "At his return, having received the authority to be king, he summoned those servants he had given the money to, so that he could find out how much they had made in business. ¹⁶ The first came forward and said, 'Master, your mina has earned ten more minas.'

¹⁷ "'Well done, good servant!' he told him. 'Because you have been faithful in a very small matter, have authority over ten towns.'

¹⁸ "The second came and said, 'Master, your mina has made five minas.'

¹⁹ "So he said to him, 'You will be over five towns.'

²⁰ "And another came and said, 'Master, here is your mina. I have kept it safe in a cloth ²¹ because I was afraid of you since you're a harsh man: you collect what you didn't deposit and reap what you didn't sow.'

²² "He told him, 'I will condemn you by what you have said, you evil servant! If you knew I was a harsh man, collecting what I didn't deposit and reaping what I didn't sow, ²³ why, then, didn't you put my money in the bank? And when I returned, I would have collected it with interest.' ²⁴ So he said to those standing there, 'Take the mina away from him and give it to the one who has ten minas.'

²⁵ "But they said to him, 'Master, he has ten minas.'

²⁶ "'I tell you, that to everyone who has, more will be given; and from the one who does not have, even what he does have will be taken away. ²⁷ But bring here these enemies of mine, who did not want me to rule over them, and slaughter them in my presence.'"

THE TRIUMPHAL ENTRY

²⁸ When he had said these things, he went on ahead, going up to Jerusalem. ²⁹ As he approached Bethphage and Bethany, at the place called the Mount of Olives, he sent two of the disciples ³⁰ and said, "Go into the village ahead of you. As you enter it, you will find a young donkey tied there, on which no one has ever sat. Untie it and bring it. ³¹ If anyone asks you, 'Why are you untying it?' say this: 'The Lord needs it.'"

³² So those who were sent left and found it just as he had told them. ³³ As they were untying the young donkey, its owners said to them, "Why are you untying the donkey?"

³⁴ "The Lord needs it," they said. ³⁵ Then they brought it to Jesus, and after throwing their clothes on the donkey, they helped Jesus get on it. ³⁶ As he was going along, they were spreading their clothes on the road. ³⁷ Now he came near the path down the Mount of Olives, and the whole crowd of the disciples began to praise God joyfully with a loud voice for all the miracles they had seen:

³⁸ Blessed is the King who comes
in the name of the Lord.
Peace in heaven
and glory in the highest heaven!

³⁹ Some of the Pharisees from the crowd told him, "Teacher, rebuke your disciples."

⁴⁰ He answered, "I tell you, if they were to keep silent, the stones would cry out."

JESUS'S LOVE FOR JERUSALEM

⁴¹ As he approached and saw the city, he wept for it, ⁴² saying, "If you knew this day what would bring peace—but now it is hidden from your eyes. ⁴³ For the days will come on you when your enemies will build a barricade around you, surround you, and hem you in on every side. ⁴⁴ They will crush you and your children among you to the ground, and they will not leave one stone on another in your midst, because you did not recognize the time when God visited you."

CLEANSING THE TEMPLE

⁴⁵ He went into the temple and began to throw out those who were selling, ⁴⁶ and he said, "It is written, my house will be a house of prayer, but you have made it a den of thieves!"

⁴⁷ Every day he was teaching in the temple. The chief priests, the scribes, and the leaders of the people were looking for a way to kill him, ⁴⁸ but they could not find a way to do it, because all the people were captivated by what they heard.

2 Chronicles 16:9

For the eyes of the Lᴏʀᴅ roam throughout the earth to show himself strong for those who are wholeheartedly devoted to him. You have been foolish in this matter. Therefore, you will have wars from now on.

James 4:13–17

OUR WILL AND GOD'S WILL

¹³ Come now, you who say, "Today or tomorrow we will travel to such and such a city and spend a year there and do business and make a profit." ¹⁴ Yet you do not know what tomorrow will bring—what your life will be! For you are like vapor that appears for a little while, then vanishes.

¹⁵ Instead, you should say, "If the Lord wills, we will live and do this or that." ¹⁶ But as it is, you boast in your arrogance. All such boasting is evil. ¹⁷ So it is sin to know the good and yet not do it.

NOTES

For this is what the Lord GOD says:
See, I myself will search for my flock and look for them.

Day 27

GRACE DAY

Use this day to pray, rest, and reflect on this week's reading, giving thanks for the grace that is ours in Christ.

> [11] "For this is what the Lord GOD says: See, I myself will search for my flock and look for them. [12] As a shepherd looks for his sheep on the day he is among his scattered flock, so I will look for my flock. I will rescue them from all the places where they have been scattered on a day of clouds and total darkness."
>
> *Ezekiel 34:11–12*

WEEKLY TRUTH

Scripture is God-breathed and true. When we memorize it, we carry the gospel with us wherever we go.

This week we will memorize the key verse for the Gospel of Luke.

"For the Son of Man has come to seek and to save the lost."

Luke 19:10

"He is not the God of the dead but of the living, because all are living to him."

Luke 20:38

THE AUTHORITY OF JESUS CHALLENGED

Luke 20

THE AUTHORITY OF JESUS CHALLENGED

¹ One day as he was teaching the people in the temple and proclaiming the good news, the chief priests and the scribes, with the elders, came ² and said to him: "Tell us, by what authority are you doing these things? Who is it who gave you this authority?"

³ He answered them, "I will also ask you a question. Tell me, ⁴ was the baptism of John from heaven or of human origin?"

⁵ They discussed it among themselves: "If we say, 'From heaven,' he will say, 'Why didn't you believe him?' ⁶ But if we say, 'Of human origin,' all the people will stone us, because they are convinced that John was a prophet." ⁷ So they answered that they did not know its origin.

⁸ And Jesus said to them, "Neither will I tell you by what authority I do these things."

THE PARABLE OF THE VINEYARD OWNER

⁹ Now he began to tell the people this parable: "A man planted a vineyard, leased it to tenant farmers, and went away for a long time. ¹⁰ At harvest time he sent a servant to the farmers so that they might give him some fruit from the vineyard. But the farmers beat him and sent him away empty-handed. ¹¹ He sent yet another servant, but they beat that one too, treated him shamefully, and sent him away empty-handed. ¹² And he sent yet a third, but they wounded this one too and threw him out.

¹³ "Then the owner of the vineyard said, 'What should I do? I will send my beloved son. Perhaps they will respect him.'

¹⁴ "But when the tenant farmers saw him, they discussed it among themselves and said, 'This is the heir. Let's kill him, so that the inheritance will be ours.' ¹⁵ So they threw him out of the vineyard and killed him.

"What then will the owner of the vineyard do to them? ¹⁶ He will come and kill those farmers and give the vineyard to others."

But when they heard this they said, "That must never happen!"

¹⁷ But he looked at them and said, "Then what is the meaning of this Scripture:

The stone that the builders rejected
has become the cornerstone?

¹⁸ Everyone who falls on that stone will be broken to pieces, but on whomever it falls, it will shatter him."

¹⁹ Then the scribes and the chief priests looked for a way to get their hands on him that very hour, because they knew he had told this parable against them, but they feared the people.

GOD AND CAESAR

²⁰ They watched closely and sent spies who pretended to be righteous, so that they could catch him in what he said, to hand him over to the governor's rule and authority. ²¹ They questioned him, "Teacher, we know that you speak and teach correctly, and you don't show partiality but teach truthfully the way of God. ²² Is it lawful for us to pay taxes to Caesar or not?"

²³ But detecting their craftiness, he said to them, ²⁴ "Show me a denarius. Whose image and inscription does it have?"

"Caesar's," they said.

²⁵ "Well then," he told them, "give to Caesar the things that are Caesar's, and to God the things that are God's."

²⁶ They were not able to catch him in what he said in public, and being amazed at his answer, they became silent.

THE SADDUCEES AND THE RESURRECTION

²⁷ Some of the Sadducees, who say there is no resurrection, came up and questioned him: ²⁸ "Teacher, Moses wrote for us that if a man's brother has a wife, and dies childless, his brother should take the wife and produce offspring for his brother. ²⁹ Now there were seven brothers. The first took a wife and died without children. ³⁰ Also the second ³¹ and the third took her. In the same way, all seven died and left no children. ³² Finally, the woman died too. ³³ In the resurrection, therefore, whose wife will the woman be? For all seven had married her."

³⁴ Jesus told them, "The children of this age marry and are given in marriage. ³⁵ But those who are counted worthy to take part in that age and in the resurrection from the dead neither marry nor are given in marriage. ³⁶ For they can no longer die, because they are like angels and are children of God, since they are children of the resurrection. ³⁷ Moses even indicated in the passage about the burning bush that the dead are raised, where he calls the Lord the God of Abraham and the God of Isaac and the God of Jacob. ³⁸ He is not the God of the dead but of the living, because all are living to him."

³⁹ Some of the scribes answered, "Teacher, you have spoken well." ⁴⁰ And they no longer dared to ask him anything.

THE QUESTION ABOUT THE CHRIST

⁴¹ Then he said to them, "How can they say that the Christ is the son of David? ⁴² For David himself says in the Book of Psalms:

The Lord declared to my Lord,
'Sit at my right hand
⁴³ until I make your enemies your footstool.'

⁴⁴ David calls him 'Lord' how then can the Christ be his son?"

WARNING AGAINST THE SCRIBES

⁴⁵ While all the people were listening, he said to his disciples, ⁴⁶ "Beware of the scribes, who want to go around in long robes and who love greetings in the marketplaces, the best seats in the synagogues, and the places of honor at banquets. ⁴⁷ They devour widows' houses and say long prayers just for show. These will receive harsher judgment."

Isaiah 26:19

Your dead will live; their bodies will rise.
Awake and sing, you who dwell in the dust!
For you will be covered with the morning dew,
and the earth will bring out the departed spirits.

I Peter 1:3–4

³ Blessed be the God and Father of our Lord Jesus Christ. Because of his great mercy he has given us new birth into a living hope through the resurrection of Jesus Christ from the dead ⁴ and into an inheritance that is imperishable, undefiled, and unfading, kept in heaven for you.

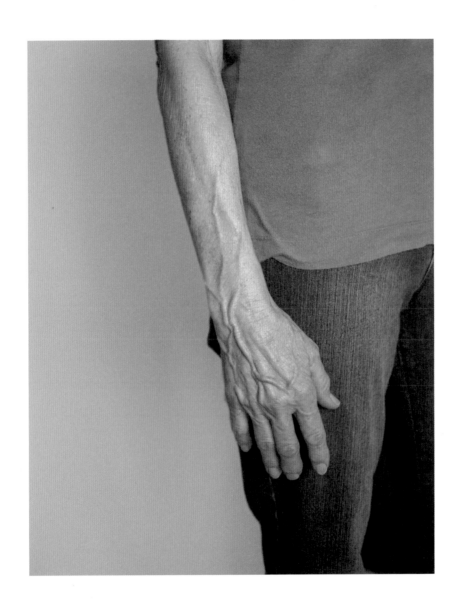

The Coming of the Son of Man

THE WIDOW'S GIFT

¹ He looked up and saw the rich dropping their offerings into the temple treasury. ² He also saw a poor widow dropping in two tiny coins. ³ "Truly I tell you," he said. "This poor widow has put in more than all of them. ⁴ For all these people have put in gifts out of their surplus, but she out of her poverty has put in all she had to live on."

DESTRUCTION OF THE TEMPLE PREDICTED

⁵ As some were talking about the temple, how it was adorned with beautiful stones and gifts dedicated to God, he said, ⁶ "These things that you see—the days will come when not one stone will be left on another that will not be thrown down."

SIGNS OF THE END OF THE AGE

⁷ "Teacher," they asked him, "so when will these things happen? And what will be the sign when these things are about to take place?"

⁸ Then he said, "Watch out that you are not deceived. For many will come in my name, saying, 'I am he,' and, 'The time is near.' Don't follow them. ⁹ When you hear of wars and rebellions, don't be alarmed. Indeed, it is necessary that these things take place first, but the end won't come right away."

¹⁰ Then he told them: "Nation will be raised up against nation, and kingdom against kingdom. ¹¹ There will be violent earthquakes, and famines and plagues in various places, and there will be terrifying sights and great signs from heaven. ¹² But before all these things, they will lay their hands on you and persecute you. They will hand you over to the synagogues and prisons, and you will be brought before kings and governors because of my name. ¹³ This will give you an opportunity to bear witness. ¹⁴ Therefore make up your minds not to prepare your defense ahead of time, ¹⁵ for I will give you such words and a wisdom that none of your adversaries will be able to resist or contradict. ¹⁶ You will even be betrayed by parents, brothers, relatives, and friends. They will kill some of you. ¹⁷ You will be hated by everyone because of my name, ¹⁸ but not a hair of your head will be lost. ¹⁹ By your endurance, gain your lives.

THE DESTRUCTION OF JERUSALEM

²⁰ "When you see Jerusalem surrounded by armies, then recognize that its desolation has come near. ²¹ Then those in Judea must flee to the mountains. Those inside the city must leave it, and those who are in the country must not enter it, ²² because these are days of vengeance to fulfill all the things that are written. ²³ Woe to pregnant women and nursing mothers in those days, for there will be great distress in the land and wrath against this people. ²⁴ They will be killed by the sword and be led captive into all the nations, and Jerusalem will be trampled by the Gentiles until the times of the Gentiles are fulfilled.

THE COMING OF THE SON OF MAN

²⁵ "Then there will be signs in the sun, moon, and stars; and there will be anguish on the earth among nations bewildered by the roaring of the sea and the waves. ²⁶ People will faint from fear and expectation of the things that are coming on the world, because the powers of the heavens will be shaken. ²⁷ Then they will see the Son of Man coming in a cloud with power and great glory. ²⁸ But when these things begin to take place, stand up and lift up your heads, because your redemption is near."

THE PARABLE OF THE FIG TREE

²⁹ Then he told them a parable: "Look at the fig tree, and all the trees. ³⁰ As soon as they put out leaves you can see for yourselves and recognize that summer is already near. ³¹ In the same way, when you see these things happening, recognize that the kingdom of God is near. ³² Truly I tell you, this generation will certainly not pass away until all things take place. ³³ Heaven and earth will pass away, but my words will never pass away.

THE NEED FOR WATCHFULNESS

³⁴ "Be on your guard, so that your minds are not dulled from carousing, drunkenness, and worries of life, or that day will come on you unexpectedly ³⁵ like a trap. For it will come on all who live on the face of the whole earth. ³⁶ But be alert at all times, praying that you may have strength to escape all these things that are going to take place and to stand before the Son of Man."

37 During the day, he was teaching in the temple, but in the evening he would go out and spend the night on what is called the Mount of Olives. 38 Then all the people would come early in the morning to hear him in the temple.

I Thessalonians 5:2–4

2 For you yourselves know very well that the day of the Lord will come just like a thief in the night. 3 When they say, "Peace and security," then sudden destruction will come upon them, like labor pains on a pregnant woman, and they will not escape. 4 But you, brothers and sisters, are not in the dark, for this day to surprise you like a thief.

Hebrews 12:25–29

25 See to it that you do not reject the one who speaks. For if they did not escape when they rejected him who warned them on earth, even less will we if we turn away from him who warns us from heaven. 26 His voice shook the earth at that time, but now he has promised, Yet once more I will shake not only the earth but also the heavens. 27 This expression, "Yet once more," indicates the removal of what can be shaken—that is, created things—so that what is not shaken might remain. 28 Therefore, since we are receiving a kingdom that cannot be shaken, let us be thankful. By it, we may serve God acceptably, with reverence and awe, 29 for our God is a consuming fire.

NOTES

date

The Plot to Kill Jesus

THE PLOT TO KILL JESUS

¹ The Festival of Unleavened Bread, which is called Passover, was approaching. ² The chief priests and the scribes were looking for a way to put him to death, because they were afraid of the people.

³ Then Satan entered Judas, called Iscariot, who was numbered among the Twelve. ⁴ He went away and discussed with the chief priests and temple police how he could hand him over to them. ⁵ They were glad and agreed to give him silver. ⁶ So he accepted the offer and started looking for a good opportunity to betray him to them when the crowd was not present.

PREPARATION FOR PASSOVER

⁷ Then the Day of Unleavened Bread came when the Passover lamb had to be sacrificed. ⁸ Jesus sent Peter and John, saying, "Go and make preparations for us to eat the Passover."

⁹ "Where do you want us to prepare it?" they asked him.

¹⁰ "Listen," he said to them, "when you've entered the city, a man carrying a water jug will meet you. Follow him into the house he enters. ¹¹ Tell the owner of the house, 'The Teacher asks you, "Where is the guest room where I can eat the Passover with my disciples?"' ¹² Then he will show you a large, furnished room upstairs. Make the preparations there."

¹³ So they went and found it just as he had told them, and they prepared the Passover.

THE FIRST LORD'S SUPPER

¹⁴ When the hour came, he reclined at the table, and the apostles with him. ¹⁵ Then he said to them, "I have fervently desired to eat this Passover with you before I suffer. ¹⁶ For I tell you, I will not eat it again until it is fulfilled in the kingdom of God." ¹⁷ Then he took a cup, and after giving thanks, he said, "Take this and share it among yourselves. ¹⁸ For I tell you, from now on I will not drink of the fruit of the vine until the kingdom of God comes."

¹⁹ And he took bread, gave thanks, broke it, gave it to them, and said, "This is my body, which is given for you. Do this in remembrance of me."

²⁰ In the same way he also took the cup after supper and said, "This cup is the new covenant in my blood, which is poured out for you. ²¹ But look, the hand of the one betraying me is at the table with me. ²² For the Son of Man will go away as it has been determined, but woe to that man by whom he is betrayed!"

²³ So they began to argue among themselves which of them it could be who was going to do it.

THE DISPUTE OVER GREATNESS

²⁴ Then a dispute also arose among them about who should be considered the greatest. ²⁵ But he said to them, "The kings of the Gentiles lord it over them, and those who have authority over them have themselves called 'Benefactors.' ²⁶ It is not to be like that among you. On the contrary, whoever is greatest among you should become like the youngest, and whoever leads, like the one serving. ²⁷ For who is greater, the one at the table or the one serving? Isn't it the one at the table? But I am among you as the one who serves. ²⁸ You are those who stood by me in my trials. ²⁹ I bestow on you a kingdom, just as my Father bestowed one on me, ³⁰ so that you may eat and drink at my table in my kingdom. And you will sit on thrones judging the twelve tribes of Israel.

PETER'S DENIAL PREDICTED

³¹ "Simon, Simon, look out. Satan has asked to sift you like wheat. ³² But I have prayed for you that your faith may not fail. And you, when you have turned back, strengthen your brothers."

³³ "Lord," he told him, "I'm ready to go with you both to prison and to death."

³⁴ "I tell you, Peter," he said, "the rooster will not crow today until you deny three times that you know me."

BE READY FOR TROUBLE

³⁵ He also said to them, "When I sent you out without money-bag, traveling bag, or sandals, did you lack anything?"

"Not a thing," they said.

³⁶ Then he said to them, "But now, whoever has a money-bag should take it, and also a traveling bag. And whoever doesn't have a sword should sell his robe and buy one. ³⁷ For I tell you, what is written must be fulfilled in me: And he was counted among the lawless. Yes, what is written about me is coming to its fulfillment."

³⁸ "Lord," they said, "look, here are two swords."

"That is enough!" he told them.

THE PRAYER IN THE GARDEN

³⁹ He went out and made his way as usual to the Mount of Olives, and the disciples followed him. ⁴⁰ When he reached the place, he told them, "Pray that you may not fall into temptation." ⁴¹ Then he withdrew from them about a stone's throw, knelt down, and began to pray, ⁴² "Father, if you are willing, take this cup away from me—nevertheless, not my will, but yours, be done."

⁴³ Then an angel from heaven appeared to him, strengthening him. ⁴⁴ Being in anguish, he prayed more fervently, and his sweat became like drops of blood falling to the ground. ⁴⁵ When he got up from prayer and came to the disciples, he found them sleeping, exhausted from their grief. ⁴⁶ "Why are you sleeping?" he asked them. "Get up and pray, so that you won't fall into temptation."

JUDAS'S BETRAYAL OF JESUS

⁴⁷ While he was still speaking, suddenly a mob came, and one of the Twelve named Judas was leading them. He came near Jesus to kiss him, ⁴⁸ but Jesus said to him, "Judas, are you betraying the Son of Man with a kiss?"

⁴⁹ When those around him saw what was going to happen, they asked, "Lord, should we strike with the sword?" ⁵⁰ Then one of them struck the high priest's servant and cut off his right ear.

⁵¹ But Jesus responded, "No more of this!" And touching his ear, he healed him. ⁵² Then Jesus said to the chief priests, temple police, and the elders who had come for him, "Have you come out with swords and clubs as if I were a criminal? ⁵³ Every day while I was with you in the temple, you never laid a hand on me. But this is your hour—and the dominion of darkness."

PETER DENIES HIS LORD

⁵⁴ They seized him, led him away, and brought him into the high priest's house. Meanwhile Peter was following at a distance. ⁵⁵ They lit a fire in the middle of the courtyard and sat down together, and Peter sat among them. ⁵⁶ When a servant saw him sitting in the light, and looked closely at him, she said, "This man was with him too."

57 But he denied it: "Woman, I don't know him."

58 After a little while, someone else saw him and said, "You're one of them too."

"Man, I am not!" Peter said.

59 About an hour later, another kept insisting, "This man was certainly with him, since he's also a Galilean."

60 But Peter said, "Man, I don't know what you're talking about!" Immediately, while he was still speaking, a rooster crowed. 61 Then the Lord turned and looked at Peter. So Peter remembered the word of the Lord, how he had said to him, "Before the rooster crows today, you will deny me three times." 62 And he went outside and wept bitterly.

JESUS MOCKED AND BEATEN

63 The men who were holding Jesus started mocking and beating him. 64 After blindfolding him, they kept asking, "Prophesy! Who was it that hit you?" 65 And they were saying many other blasphemous things to him.

JESUS FACES THE SANHEDRIN

66 When daylight came, the elders of the people, both the chief priests and the scribes, convened and brought him before their Sanhedrin. 67 They said, "If you are the Messiah, tell us."

But he said to them, "If I do tell you, you will not believe. 68 And if I ask you, you will not answer. 69 But from now on, the Son of Man will be seated at the right hand of the power of God."

70 They all asked, "Are you, then, the Son of God?"

And he said to them, "You say that I am."

71 "Why do we need any more testimony," they said, "since we've heard it ourselves from his mouth?"

Deuteronomy 16:1–8
THE FESTIVAL OF PASSOVER

1 "Set aside the month of Abib and observe the Passover to the LORD your God, because the LORD your God brought you out of Egypt by night in the month of Abib. 2 Sacrifice to the LORD your God a Passover animal from the herd or flock in the place where the LORD chooses to have his name dwell. 3 Do not eat leavened bread with it. For seven days you are to eat unleavened bread with it, the bread of hardship—because you left the land of Egypt in a hurry—so that you may remember for the rest of your life the day you left the land of Egypt. 4 No yeast is to be found anywhere in your territory for seven days, and none of the meat you sacrifice in the evening of the first day is to remain until morning. 5 You are not to sacrifice the Passover animal in any of the towns the LORD your God is giving you. 6 Sacrifice the Passover animal only at the place where the LORD your God chooses to have his name dwell. Do this in the evening as the sun sets at the same time of day you departed from Egypt. 7 You are to cook and eat it in the place the LORD your God chooses, and you are to return to your tents in the morning. 8 Eat unleavened bread for six days. On the seventh day there is to be a solemn assembly to the LORD your God; do not do any work."

Galatians 1:3–5

3 Grace to you and peace from God the Father and our Lord Jesus Christ, 4 who gave himself for our sins to rescue us from this present evil age, according to the will of our God and Father. 5 To him be the glory forever and ever. Amen.

NOTES   *date*

The Death of Jesus

Luke 23

JESUS FACES PILATE

[1] Then their whole assembly rose up and brought him before Pilate. [2] They began to accuse him, saying, "We found this man misleading our nation, opposing payment of taxes to Caesar, and saying that he himself is the Messiah, a king."

[3] So Pilate asked him, "Are you the king of the Jews?"

He answered him, "You say so."

[4] Pilate then told the chief priests and the crowds, "I find no grounds for charging this man."

[5] But they kept insisting, "He stirs up the people, teaching throughout all Judea, from Galilee where he started even to here."

JESUS FACES HEROD ANTIPAS

[6] When Pilate heard this, he asked if the man was a Galilean. [7] Finding that he was under Herod's jurisdiction, he sent him to Herod, who was also in Jerusalem during those days. [8] Herod was very glad to see Jesus; for a long time he had wanted to see him because he had heard about him and was hoping to see some miracle performed by him. [9] So he kept asking him questions, but Jesus did not answer him. [10] The chief priests and the scribes stood by, vehemently accusing him. [11] Then Herod, with his soldiers, treated him with contempt, mocked him, dressed him in bright clothing, and sent him back to Pilate. [12] That very day Herod and Pilate became friends. Previously, they had been enemies.

JESUS OR BARABBAS

[13] Pilate called together the chief priests, the leaders, and the people, [14] and said to them, "You have brought me this man as one who misleads the people. But in fact, after examining him in your presence, I have found no grounds to charge this man with those things you accuse him of. [15] Neither has Herod, because he sent him back to us. Clearly, he has done nothing to deserve death. [16] Therefore, I will have him whipped and then release him."

[18] Then they all cried out together, "Take this man away! Release Barabbas to us!" [19] (He had been thrown into prison for a rebellion that had taken place in the city, and for murder.)

²⁰ Wanting to release Jesus, Pilate addressed them again, ²¹ but they kept shouting, "Crucify! Crucify him!"

²² A third time he said to them, "Why? What has this man done wrong? I have found in him no grounds for the death penalty. Therefore, I will have him whipped and then release him."

²³ But they kept up the pressure, demanding with loud voices that he be crucified, and their voices won out. ²⁴ So Pilate decided to grant their demand ²⁵ and released the one they were asking for, who had been thrown into prison for rebellion and murder. But he handed Jesus over to their will.

THE WAY TO THE CROSS

²⁶ As they led him away, they seized Simon, a Cyrenian, who was coming in from the country, and laid the cross on him to carry behind Jesus. ²⁷ A large crowd of people followed him, including women who were mourning and lamenting him. ²⁸ But turning to them, Jesus said, "Daughters of Jerusalem, do not weep for me, but weep for yourselves and your children. ²⁹ Look, the days are coming when they will say, 'Blessed are the women without children, the wombs that never bore, and the breasts that never nursed!' ³⁰ Then they will begin to say to the mountains, 'Fall on us!' and to the hills, 'Cover us!' ³¹ For if they do these things when the wood is green, what will happen when it is dry?"

CRUCIFIED BETWEEN TWO CRIMINALS

³² Two others—criminals—were also led away to be executed with him. ³³ When they arrived at the place called The Skull, they crucified him there, along with the criminals, one on the right and one on the left. ³⁴ Then Jesus said, "Father, forgive them, because they do not know what they are doing." And they divided his clothes and cast lots.

³⁵ The people stood watching, and even the leaders were scoffing: "He saved others; let him save himself if this is God's Messiah, the Chosen One!" ³⁶ The soldiers also mocked him. They came offering him sour wine ³⁷ and said, "If you are the King of the Jews, save yourself!"

³⁸ An inscription was above him: This Is the King of the Jews.

[39] Then one of the criminals hanging there began to yell insults at him: "Aren't you the Messiah? Save yourself and us!"

[40] But the other answered, rebuking him: "Don't you even fear God, since you are undergoing the same punishment? [41] We are punished justly, because we're getting back what we deserve for the things we did, but this man has done nothing wrong." [42] Then he said, "Jesus, remember me when you come into your kingdom."

[43] And he said to him, "Truly I tell you, today you will be with me in paradise."

THE DEATH OF JESUS

[44] It was now about noon, and darkness came over the whole land until three, [45] because the sun's light failed. The curtain of the sanctuary was split down the middle. [46] And Jesus called out with a loud voice, "Father, into your hands I entrust my spirit." Saying this, he breathed his last.

[47] When the centurion saw what happened, he began to glorify God, saying, "This man really was righteous!" [48] All the crowds that had gathered for this spectacle, when they saw what had taken place, went home, striking their chests. [49] But all who knew him, including the women who had followed him from Galilee, stood at a distance, watching these things.

THE BURIAL OF JESUS

[50] There was a good and righteous man named Joseph, a member of the Sanhedrin, [51] who had not agreed with their plan and action. He was from Arimathea, a Judean town, and was looking forward to the kingdom of God. [52] He approached Pilate and asked for Jesus's body. [53] Taking it down, he wrapped it in fine linen and placed it in a tomb cut into the rock, where no one had ever been placed. [54] It was the preparation day, and the Sabbath was about to begin. [55] The women who had come with him from Galilee followed along and observed the tomb and how his body was placed. [56] Then they returned and prepared spices and perfumes. And they rested on the Sabbath according to the commandment.

Psalm 38:20–21

[20] Those who repay evil for good
attack me for pursuing good.

[21] LORD, do not abandon me;
my God, do not be far from me.

Acts 4:23–31

PRAYER FOR BOLDNESS

[23] After they were released, they went to their own people and reported everything the chief priests and the elders had said to them. [24] When they heard this, they raised their voices together to God and said, "Master, you are the one who made the heaven, the earth, and the sea, and everything in them. [25] You said through the Holy Spirit, by the mouth of our father David your servant:

Why do the Gentiles rage
and the peoples plot futile things?
[26] The kings of the earth take their stand
and the rulers assemble together
against the Lord and against his Messiah.

[27] "For, in fact, in this city both Herod and Pontius Pilate, with the Gentiles and the people of Israel, assembled together against your holy servant Jesus, whom you anointed, [28] to do whatever your hand and your will had predestined to take place. [29] And now, Lord, consider their threats, and grant that your servants may speak your word with all boldness, [30] while you stretch out your hand for healing, and signs and wonders are performed through the name of your holy servant Jesus." [31] When they had prayed, the place where they were assembled was shaken, and they were all filled with the Holy Spirit and began to speak the word of God boldly.

Day 33

The Reality of the Risen Jesus

RESURRECTION MORNING

¹ On the first day of the week, very early in the morning, they came to the tomb, bringing the spices they had prepared. ² They found the stone rolled away from the tomb. ³ They went in but did not find the body of the Lord Jesus. ⁴ While they were perplexed about this, suddenly two men stood by them in dazzling clothes. ⁵ So the women were terrified and bowed down to the ground.

"Why are you looking for the living among the dead?" asked the men. ⁶ "He is not here, but he has risen! Remember how he spoke to you when he was still in Galilee, ⁷ saying, 'It is necessary that the Son of Man be betrayed into the hands of sinful men, be crucified, and rise on the third day'?" ⁸ And they remembered his words.

⁹ Returning from the tomb, they reported all these things to the Eleven and to all the rest. ¹⁰ Mary Magdalene, Joanna, Mary the mother of James, and the other women with them were telling the apostles these things. ¹¹ But these words seemed like nonsense to them, and they did not believe the women. ¹² Peter, however, got up and ran to the tomb. When he stooped to look in, he saw only the linen cloths. So he went away, amazed at what had happened.

THE EMMAUS DISCIPLES

¹³ Now that same day two of them were on their way to a village called Emmaus, which was about seven miles from Jerusalem. ¹⁴ Together they were discussing everything that had taken place. ¹⁵ And while they were discussing and arguing, Jesus himself came near and began to walk along with them. ¹⁶ But they were prevented from recognizing him. ¹⁷ Then he asked them, "What is this dispute that you're having with each other as you are walking?" And they stopped walking and looked discouraged.

¹⁸ The one named Cleopas answered him, "Are you the only visitor in Jerusalem who doesn't know the things that happened there in these days?"

¹⁹ "What things?" he asked them.

So they said to him, "The things concerning Jesus of Nazareth, who was a prophet powerful in action and speech before God and all the people, ²⁰ and how our chief priests and leaders handed him over to be sentenced to death, and they crucified him. ²¹ But we were hoping that he was the one who was about to redeem Israel. Besides all this, it's the third day since these things happened. ²² Moreover, some women from our group astounded us. They arrived early at the tomb, ²³ and when they didn't find his body, they came and reported that they had seen a vision of angels who said he was alive. ²⁴ Some of those who were with us went to the tomb and found it just as the women had said, but they didn't see him."

²⁵ He said to them, "How foolish and slow you are to believe all that the prophets have spoken! ²⁶ Wasn't it necessary for the Messiah to suffer these things and enter into his glory?" ²⁷ Then beginning with Moses and all the Prophets, he interpreted for them the things concerning himself in all the Scriptures.

²⁸ They came near the village where they were going, and he gave the impression that he was going farther. ²⁹ But they urged him, "Stay with us, because it's almost evening, and now the day is almost over." So he went in to stay with them.

³⁰ It was as he reclined at the table with them that he took the bread, blessed and broke it, and gave it to them. ³¹ Then their eyes were opened, and they recognized him, but he disappeared from their sight. ³² They said to each other, "Weren't our hearts burning within us while he was talking with us on the road and explaining the Scriptures to us?" ³³ That very hour they got up and returned to Jerusalem. They found the Eleven and those with them gathered together, ³⁴ who said, "The Lord has truly been raised and has appeared to Simon!" ³⁵ Then they began to describe what had happened on the road and how he was made known to them in the breaking of the bread.

THE REALITY OF THE RISEN JESUS

³⁶ As they were saying these things, he himself stood in their midst. He said to them, "Peace to you!" ³⁷ But they were startled and terrified and thought they were seeing a ghost. ³⁸ "Why are you troubled?" he asked them. "And why do doubts arise in your hearts? ³⁹ Look at my hands and my feet, that it is I myself! Touch me and see, because a ghost does

not have flesh and bones as you can see I have." [40] Having said this, he showed them his hands and feet. [41] But while they still were amazed and in disbelief because of their joy, he asked them, "Do you have anything here to eat?" [42] So they gave him a piece of a broiled fish, [43] and he took it and ate in their presence.

[44] He told them, "These are my words that I spoke to you while I was still with you—that everything written about me in the Law of Moses, the Prophets, and the Psalms must be fulfilled." [45] Then he opened their minds to understand the Scriptures. [46] He also said to them, "This is what is written: The Messiah would suffer and rise from the dead the third day, [47] and repentance for forgiveness of sins would be proclaimed in his name to all the nations, beginning at Jerusalem. [48] You are witnesses of these things. [49] And look, I am sending you what my Father promised. As for you, stay in the city until you are empowered from on high."

THE ASCENSION OF JESUS

[50] Then he led them out to the vicinity of Bethany, and lifting up his hands he blessed them. [51] And while he was blessing them, he left them and was carried up into heaven. [52] After worshiping him, they returned to Jerusalem with great joy. [53] And they were continually in the temple praising God.

Philippians 2:7–11

[7] Instead he emptied himself
by assuming the form of a servant,
taking on the likeness of humanity.
And when he had come as a man,
[8] he humbled himself by becoming obedient
to the point of death—
even to death on a cross.
[9] For this reason God highly exalted him
and gave him the name
that is above every name,
[10] so that at the name of Jesus
every knee will bow—
in heaven and on earth
and under the earth—
[11] and every tongue will confess
that Jesus Christ is Lord,
to the glory of God the Father.

1 John 1:1–3

PROLOGUE: OUR DECLARATION

[1] What was from the beginning, what we have heard, what we have seen with our eyes, what we have observed and have touched with our hands, concerning the word of life— [2] that life was revealed, and we have seen it and we testify and declare to you the eternal life that was with the Father and was revealed to us— [3] what we have seen and heard we also declare to you, so that you may also have fellowship with us; and indeed our fellowship is with the Father and with his Son Jesus Christ.

NOTES

date

This timeline is an approximation of the chronology of Jesus's post-resurrection appearances based on New Testament references.

Mary Magdalene
JN 20:11–18

Resurrection Sunday

Two women, possibly Mary, mother of James, and Salome
MK 16:12

Cleopas and one companion on the road to Emmaus
LK 24:13–35

Simon Peter
LK 24:34

Small gathering of disciples, without Thomas
JN 20:19–23

8 Days Later

The eleven remaining disciples, including Thomas
JN 20:26–29

Over the Next
Few Weeks

 Seven disciples at the Sea of Tiberias
JN 21:1–23

Five hundred believers at
one time, then James
1CO 15:6–7

 The disciples on a mountain in Galilee
MT 28:16–17

 The disciples in Jerusalem before Jesus
gave the Great Commission and ascended
into heaven
LK 24:49–53

The 40th
Day

Your dead will live; their bodies will rise.
Awake and sing, you who dwell in the dust!

Day 34

GRACE DAY

Use this day to pray, rest, and reflect on this week's reading, giving thanks for the grace that is ours in Christ.

Your dead will live; their bodies will rise.
Awake and sing, you who dwell in the dust!
For you will be covered with the morning dew,
and the earth will bring out the departed spirits.

Isaiah 26:19

Day 35

WEEKLY TRUTH

Scripture is God-breathed and true. When we memorize it, we carry the gospel with us wherever we go.

This week we will memorize the thief's confession to Jesus on the cross.

Then he said, "Jesus, remember me when you come into your kingdom."

Luke 23:42

THEMES IN LUKE: REFLECTION

Look over the themes you marked as you read. Use this space to retrace, reflect on, and pray through the themes you observed in the Gospel of Luke.

1 *The presence of the Holy Spirit*

2 *Prayer and teaching on prayer*

3 *The importance
of faith*

4 *Joy in God's
salvation*

5 *The kingdom
of God*

DOWNLOAD THE APP

STOP BY
shereadstruth.com

SHOP
shopshereadstruth.com

SEND A NOTE
hello@shereadstruth.com

SHARE
#SheReadsTruth

SHE READS TRUTH *is a worldwide community of women who read God's Word together every day.*

Founded in 2012, She Reads Truth invites women of all ages to engage with Scripture through daily reading plans, online conversation led by a vibrant community of contributors, and offline resources created at the intersection of beauty, goodness, and Truth.

WHERE DID I STUDY?

- O HOME
- O OFFICE
- O COFFEE SHOP
- O CHURCH
- O A FRIEND'S HOUSE
- O OTHER

WHAT WAS I LISTENING TO?

ARTIST:

SONG:

PLAYLIST:

WHEN DID I STUDY?

MORNING

AFTERNOON

NIGHT

What did I learn?

WHAT WAS HAPPENING IN MY LIFE?

WHAT WAS HAPPENING IN THE WORLD?

MONTH	DAY	YEAR

END DATE